MW01286220

-- BLINK --

Finding Strength in the Struggle

CHRISTY HARDIN

WESTBOW
PRESS®
A DIVISION OF THOMAS NELSON
& ZONDERVAN

Shannon,
I am so thankful for your friendship and support. You are an inspiration.

love,
Christy

WestBow Press books may be ordered through booksellers or by contacting:

WestBow Press
A Division of Thomas Nelson & Zondervan
1663 Liberty Drive
Bloomington, IN 47403
www.westbowpress.com
1 (866) 928-1240

ISBN: 978-1-9736-8092-5 (sc)
ISBN: 978-1-9736-8091-8 (hc)
ISBN: 978-1-9736-8094-9 (e)

Library of Congress Control Number: 2019919567

Print information available on the last page.

WestBow Press rev. date: 12/2/2019

TO MY MOM

For your unconditional love and support.

TO MY HUSBAND

For being my best friend, biggest supporter, and loving me so well.

Foreword

Our world these days is filled with texts, emojis and short-cuts, and even with the multitude of self-help gurus and books, deep thought and reflection seem to be in short supply. We listen to each other mostly in anticipation of what we are going to say next. Having just retired from teaching high school, I can say that the simple art of conversation and reflection is somewhat of an outdated practice.

When my niece told me that she was going to write a book, I knew right away that she could do it, but when would she have time with such a large family? Time for reflection? How and when? Before long, she was ready for a bit of editing from her English teacher aunt. I knew her story, or so I thought, and was anxious to see how she crafted the story of her life.

Christy unveils her engaging story with totally relatable stories along with suspenseful moments that will shock and amaze readers. I know you'll enjoy following her journey just as I did and still do to this day!

Mrs. Daphne Copeland Norton

Acknowledgments

I have to start by thanking my amazing husband, Rich. From reading early drafts to encouraging me to continue, he gave me great advice and was as important to this books completion as I was. It was fun walking down memory lane with you, my love.

Thank you to my mom, Phyllis for reading, rereading, making suggestions, helping me get through those tough chapters, and for always being there cheering me on. There are no words to describe how much I admire and respect you. Your love got me through and no matter what the future holds, I will always be by your side.

To my wonderful Aunt Daphne, for spending hours editing, talking through ideas, and for being a constant support for me through the years, no matter what. I love you and thank you so much for everything.

My twin, my first love who was sent to save me, my Ashley, thank you for forgiving me for all of my mistakes along the way as we grew up together. Your determination, strength, and love for life is inspiring and I know you will continue to change the world. I love you, Bubbie.

To my children, for bringing love, loudness, and laughter into our home. Your patience through this process has been wonderful and I love each of you so much.

Growing up with a sister that is eighteen months older than you can prove to have many adventures. Jennifer, I wouldn't change those summers on the river shore with you for anything. Thank you for your encouragement and support through the years.

There are friends in life that become family and I am so thankful for mine. To my dear Awaken family who have stood by me through life and this process, providing prayers and support, thank you. I love each of you dearly.

There are times when you come across someone from your past that plays an integral part of your future. When my childhood friend began her company, I knew that she was the one who would help me make this dream into a reality. Thank you to my proofreader and editor, Mandy with BluProof for your brilliant ideas and suggestions.

Contents

CHAPTER 1
D-Day

Blink.
Blink.
Blink.

I sit here watching the cursor blinking, and there are a million things I want to say, but I am just staring at this black line going away and coming back.

An instant. One second. That is how long each blink lasts. If I watch it long enough, I can start to hear my heartbeat to the rhythm of the blink. If I am not careful, I could sit here for a long time just watching this thing go away and come back. It always comes back at the same time, the same speed, and the same size. I find myself counting in threes.

One. Two. Three.
One. Two. Three.

It doesn't matter where I turn, self-help books, church sermons, leadership seminars, etc., the magical number seems to be three. If you follow these three steps, your life will be transformed. If you make these three changes, your life will be awesome. If you buy these three supplements, your health will be drastically improved.

If you read these three books, you will find the success you desire. Somehow, we buy into the if we do x, y, and z, then we can obtain the feeling, thing, or accomplishment that we are searching for.

Somehow, it has become normal to leave little room for God to speak to us and instead take the word of someone else on how we can have a better life. We yearn for guidance through books, sermons, podcasts, blogs, vlogs, social media opinions, and others' interpretations of scripture. We focus so much on listening for the three key steps that are coming, while writing like crazy to fill in the blanks of the sermon handout, that we could be missing what God is actually trying to speak to us. I think we do this because we live in an age where answers can be found in moments just by completing an internet search. The thought of waiting to hear from God, not knowing how long that might take, is difficult. Please don't think that I am saying that sermons, podcasts, blogs, etc., are not important, because they are. We need as much Jesus as possible. In this fast-paced, want it now, overscheduled and overcommitted life, how much time is set aside to listen to Him and study His word? Are we listening so hard for those three steps that we miss what God is trying to show us? What He has for me to hear is not the same as what He has for you. While I am not trying to take anything away from or downplay the importance of the local church or pastors, churchgoers must realize that God is speaking through His spirit-filled Word. It is through 1) praying, 2) reading His Word, and 3) listening for His guidance, that we are able to make the decisions and choose the paths for us as individuals.

Three steps.

See how easy it is to do that?! I truly believe those three steps are the foundation of everything we do, but each step can be so hard.

It is in this moment of authenticity, of soul searching, that I realize that I am waiting for the blinking to stop, remain steady, or just disappear. With each blink, I feel like I am walking toward quicksand. There comes a time when the quicksand is approaching faster, and one step is a little harder than the last, endlessly waiting to become frozen in the sand, feeling unable to take another step. Then, surprisingly, the next step happens, and the next, and slowly the quicksand does not seem so hard to navigate.

Maybe you can relate. Maybe you are just starting to step in the sand. Maybe you are already stuck in the sand. Or, maybe you just climbed out of the sand and are back on solid ground. No matter where you are, just keep moving, even if a little bit, so that you do not get stuck. Each part of your journey starts with that first step. Not three steps. Just one step.

Have you ever been in one of those doctor's offices where you can feel the weight of their daily appointments? Delivering diagnosis after diagnosis to parents seeking answers for their children or for adults looking for answers for themselves. This particular office was comfortable and had a variety of seating options and toys to occupy children, and on this particular day, I was there to receive the results from a series of testing that would lead to some answers for one of my children, Molly. The doctor explained that the testing and evaluations indicated that she has Attention Deficit Hyperactivity Disorder (ADHD), Oppositional Defiant Disorder (ODD), and Intermittent Explosive Disorder (IED). I went in armed with my smile and humor (I can be quite the comedian when the pressure is on), my pad of paper, and a pretty accurate expectation of what was coming. With the suggestions and help from the doctor, a treatment plan was crafted, there were steps to take with the school, and there was a sense of relief. I left feeling confident that my husband, Rich, and I could help Molly through this patch of quicksand and back onto solid ground.

Oppositional Defiant Disorder was something that was new for our family, but we have become more familiar as time passes. Molly is our petite, blonde, curly-haired, blue-eyed ball of energy. If you are imagining a firecracker exploding, then you have just imagined what an ODD or IED, or a combination of the two, outburst may look like from our daughter. Never underestimate the power, strength, and determination of a six-year-old. We have been working with a therapist using cognitive behavior techniques. Our bag of tricks is growing, and we are learning all about consistency, positive reinforcement, responsibility charts, and slow breathing, but the hardest one is not reacting to the outbursts.

Several months later, I found myself in the same office, with the same doctor, for a different child. This time felt different. Although I was pretty sure of the diagnosis that was coming for our daughter, Andrea, I was not prepared to hear it. In fact, I had done minimal research on the topic and felt kind of like sticking my head in the sand instead of walking through it. You know, if you don't know then you can just ignore it. Once there was a diagnosis, then ignoring it would be impossible.

The doctor was professional as we were going through the results. She spent some length explaining the process in detail and how they use a variety of testing measures and answered my questions. She started with ADHD, which I suspected, and then moved on to ODD. Both of these were things that I had been researching and working with Molly on, so I felt confident that I could find ways to help Andrea as well. (Every time I hear ODD, I immediately think "You down with ODD, yeah you know me!" and then that classic song, with my added twist, gets stuck in my head thanks to "Naughty by Nature." I digress.)

This is when time stopped and everything changed in an instant. D-Day. Diagnosis Day. The doctor stopped talking, leaned in with her elbows on her knees, and reviewed the last portion of the testing results and her diagnosis. Autism Spectrum Disorder (ASD) – Level 1 - formally known as Asperger's. I am embarrassed to admit that I didn't even know that there were different levels.

Armed with my pen and paper, I was ready for my three steps for transformation for the tools to best help Andrea. The doctor explained that each child is different and her treatment plan will be individualized to her needs. The first step was to call her pediatrician to include him in the process and plan. She also explained there are a million hoops that we will have to jump through in this process and even more red tape that is hard to navigate. She went on to say that the most effective initial treatment plan would be finding a location for Applied Behavior Analysis (ABA) therapy, quickly followed by an almost apologetic explanation of the shortage of therapists in our area. Often there is an extensive waiting list, and it is best to find anyone that can see us, she said.

Here enters in the first encounter with the red tape process. There has to be an official diagnosis from a psychologist in order to qualify for the therapy needed. Okay, we did that. It would make sense for that report to be enough, but the insurance requires documentation from a medical doctor stating there is a medical necessity for the ABA therapy. The medical doctor, who is unable to provide the diagnosis, is the one who must provide a statement explaining the medical necessity. We are extremely thankful to have an amazing pediatrician, and this is not a problem. It just seems unnecessary to someone on the outside looking in, but nobody asked for my opinion when they were making the rules.

The next step, or obstacle, is finding a good place for ABA therapy. Clearly, there is a huge shortage of therapists providing these types of services. I can only assume this shortage is the direct result of the increasing number of diagnoses, those seeking treatment, and the ever-changing insurance policies and rules. Andrea is currently on the waitlist with four companies, all with six to nine-months-long waiting lists, potentially longer, depending on how the current children are progressing or who moves from the area.

Okay, step one and two are written down as I await number three. Reality starts setting in. There aren't just three easy, definite steps. The rest of the steps will unfold over time. The next official step was to contact the school, which would lead to more and more steps.

So many steps. So much quicksand fast approaching.

My question for the doctor, which I shocked myself with only having one question come to mind, was do we tell our precious girl that she will forever have this diagnosis. Her answer helped me as much as it would help our daughter. She paused for a moment and let me know it would not be of benefit to tell her at this point. Andrea knew that she came for testing, so we would tell her that through all of this testing, we have learned a lot about her. She is brilliant and likes to know what is going on, but she is learning that it is okay to not always know what to do or how to do something. Part of what we will work through is how we can best help her navigate this together. We see that she has some areas that she would like to work on, and we will help her through each step of the way. This validates her feelings and removes the burden of having to figure it out on her own. As time progresses, and with the help of her trusted therapist, the appropriate opportunity will present itself to let her know. The psychologist let me know how important it was to get her into ABA therapy as soon as possible because the earlier the treatment, the higher success. If we were on a waitlist for ABA therapy, then she should start with cognitive behavioral therapy in the meantime.

Overwhelmed. That was all I could think.

When I say everything changed, I don't literally mean everything. Our love for her, our desire to do everything in our power to help her succeed, her love for God and sharing her faith with *everyone* (and I do mean everyone), her ability to succeed in school, and many, many other things did not change. What changed was our understanding of how we parent her, how the school will help her, which route we will go as far as medications, and an "aha moment" of all the signs that we missed up to this point of her diagnosis.

Bam.
There it was.
Instant mom guilt.

The appointment was over, and I left feeling numb with my list of things to do, many more than the three I had become accustomed to, and sat in my van. I sat there staring into space for the longest time, replaying each missed sign, each question mark with behavior that was just a little different, thinking about all the times I said "look at me when I am talking to you," the times I cut her off when she was telling me the forty-eight thousandth detail of a movie she watched three years ago, and, the real gut punch, thinking about interrupting and stopping her during her dinnertime prayer (I mean, it was after fifteen minutes, but still!), as she prayed specifically for every person she had ever met and even some she had not met yet.

Hard. Everything about this is hard.

I called Rich, who was at home with our children, and explained what the doctor said and our next steps. I sent a message to a friend who had been praying for our family and who also happens to be a fantastic special education teacher and will be a great resource. When she asked how I was doing with the diagnosis, I decided to be completely transparent and share the thoughts that were going through my mind. How could I have missed the signs for so long? As her mother, shouldn't I have been more aware of what was going on? If I had only noticed sooner, she could have started treatment or ABA therapy earlier. How badly did I mess up not getting her the help she needs before now? She stopped me in my tracks. She reminded me that it does no good to look backwards and that we must keep moving forward. The fact that we can now get her the help she needs will be life-changing for her and that her foundation, built on love and a desire to love the Lord, will not be shaken. She will use her gifts and talents to proclaim God's love in a way that no one else can.

You see, even before Andrea was walking, she was preaching. She would stand on the chair and give sermons and share Bible stories she learned through movies, reading Bible stories at night with Rich, and at our local church. Her ability to memorize and share, with proper enunciation nonetheless, is amazing. She has announced that our family would be growing for three separate pregnancies (each before we knew or had any indication that a baby was coming) and predicted the date of delivery accurately for two of those births. She has been our little pastor profit since she was able to talk, and those gifts can be built upon to share the Word of God with everyone she meets. That is something that can never be taken away from her.

On her first day of public school, which was in third grade after switching from a private school, I asked her how her day was. Instead of telling me about the school, new friends and the playground, she was extremely upset and said that she was absolutely shocked that there were four students in her class who were not Christians. Her mission in life is to share about Jesus without fear of judgment or ridicule. When I think back to her determined face, telling us that they may not know Jesus yet, but they would soon and hopefully they would be able to tell their parents also, I see the impact Andrea is having, and I beam with pride.

I am not super proud to admit that I have had friends for years and am not certain if they are Christians. This girl goes boldly and makes it a priority in every relationship she has to make sure they know Jesus. Yes, her differences make her unique, but they do not, and will not ever, make her any less important. Our goal is to give her the tools she needs to remain confident in who she is.

God knew Andrea before she was formed. He knew how tall she would be, her eye color, where each freckle would be, and certainly knew about this eventual diagnosis. God also knew my ability to be able to handle this situation, with the support of Rich and our families, and His timing is always perfect. While I did not necessarily feel prepared for this diagnosis, I was certainly more prepared and in a better life situation to handle this than I was with my first child. Getting this diagnosis for my child in my late 30s versus in my late teens is what enabled me to have the mindset to have the goal for her to remain confident. In order to fully understand my present life, understanding my past is extremely important.

CHAPTER 2
Twists and Turns

I keep thinking about how I could possibly sum up nearly thirty years of life into one chapter. As I think back, I can almost see the different chapters where life happened and new chapters began. To start, I grew up in a loving home with parents who were married. We were a middle-class family, and both of my parents worked outside of the home. As I look back, I never saw how hard they worked to ensure that we never lacked for anything. There was one time we begged for happy meals and really thought the world was going to end because we didn't get them. They never let on that money was tight or discussed problems in front of us, that I remember. I have a sister who is 18 months older than me, and our childhood was filled with summers at our grandparents' farm, trips to Tennessee to see our parents' best friends, annual beach vacations, Disney World trips, Friday night pizza nights with a house full of our friends before the football game, softball games, cheering practices, and growing up with our next door neighbor, who became like another sister to me.

When I was 15 years old, I got my first job at Roses Discount Store, and shortly after that began my second job at Pizza Hut with several of my friends. At one point, my dad picked up a second job delivering pizzas at night to help bring in additional income. Wonderful friends. Jobs that were fun. Attending school with many of the same friends I had had since kindergarten. Life was great. The summer was filled with pranks, ridiculous ideas that seemed so funny at the time, band camp, and more laughter than you could imagine.

It was my freshman year of high school that we moved into a larger house so that my grandparents could move in with us. While I had a somewhat difficult transition, I was always thankful to have such loving and involved grandparents. My friends called them Grandma and Granddad, and my parents became Mom and Dad to most of them, as well. Our house was always open for friends to come over and often spend the night.

The summer of my sixteenth year was what I call the end of my adolescent naivety. I had the brilliant idea that it would be fun to try some weed. I found out about a distant friend who had a connection and decided that a little dime bag would be a perfect way to start the weekend. I drove up to my friend's house, and this guy walked out to bring it to me. Later that evening, he met up with me, and from that day forward, life was never the same.

That decision led me to my first boyfriend, who would introduce me to a world I had no idea even existed. I became a master at lying to my parents to keep them from knowing the truth. My Friday nights filled with laughter soon became nights driving around with tear-stained eyes, looking at the different drug houses for him. His addiction was worse than I knew, and the substances were many. It became my goal in life to save him, and I just knew that if I loved him enough, I could make him stop.

My obsession to make sure he was okay pushed my friends away and distanced me from my parents because I truly hated lying to them. The truth was just too hard to admit. His controlling nature and sheer size was intimidating, and he made it known that he did not approve of me having male friends. Over time, I cut myself off from my female friends as well because it was too hard to admit that I was in love with an addict.

When I was seventeen and a senior in high school, I had plans to attend Virginia Tech, my dream school and where my sister was already a student. I was eager to get ahead and was enrolled in one college class while I was still in high school. School had always been a priority for our family and I was set to graduate with honors. Of course, the idea of me going away to a school so far away from home did not go over well with my boyfriend. There would be no way for me to continue to cover for and save him, and he would not be able to control my environment any longer.

Being the brilliant teenager that I was, I had set boundaries for myself that I would not cross. It was okay, in my mind, if I drank and smoked weed, as long as I didn't partake in any of the "hard" drugs. My boyfriend quickly became bored with that and wanted something more, which led to his usage of many other substances. There were times that I would sit in the car outside of a drug house waiting for him to come out, sometimes for hours. One night after waiting for him outside in the car for four hours, I had the courage to bust into one of the houses. I convinced myself that he was not okay and that I must save him. Without even knocking, I went to the door and kicked it, causing it to swing wide open. I entered the home terrified, yet filled with adrenaline as I stood face to face with his dealer. That night, I had my first encounter with the inside of a drug house. I replay that night in my mind as I think about what could have happened as I stood there. I looked around seeing cocaine piled on the table. It happened so fast and slow in my mind all at once. As quickly as the door swung open, there was a very angry man who grabbed me and I was held at gunpoint for entering his home.

Thankfully, I had gone to the ATM and had cash and was able to buy my way out of the house. Instead of calling my parents from the payphone, I sat in his car crying. He watched it happen and did nothing. He was so high that my safety was not a concern to him; instead he just sat there staring at me. How did I get here? How did I go from being on top of the world to feeling like I was in the lowest part? You would think that nearly being killed, being exposed to this dangerous and potentially deadly world, would be enough for me to leave. In my mind, if I left, then I could not save him. I became addicted to trying to save him and it was all that I could focus on. Every time he chose to get high, that meant that I was failing. In my mind, his addiction became a battle that I was fighting alone because he was not ready or at a point where he could fight himself. I lost myself trying to save someone who did not want to be saved.

That same year, I missed my own birthday party. My parents went out of their way to throw me a nice birthday party, and I was too busy trying to rescue him that I did not even bother to come home for it. That first look of disappointment on my parents' faces is something that I will never forget. Of course I could not tell them the real reason why I missed the party. I had built up this grand web of lies covering the tracks and evidence of his addiction.

Soon after that, I became pregnant. Seventeen and pregnant with a man who is a drug addict with no stability is not the ideal place to be, at any age really. I was in high school with a part-time job to support his drug habit, while pretending I was so happy with him and that everything was perfect. When I finally got the nerve to tell my parents about the baby, I decided to go to my moms' office when she was working late and break it to her there. The moment she saw me, she knew and asked me how far along I was. The conversation that night with my parents was difficult, and it was hard to look them in the eyes because I could not comprehend the disappointment they must have felt.

I did not know how it would work, how I could possibly afford to care for myself, much less a baby. The grace and love shown to me by my parents was unlike any other, and they never thought twice about helping me. Well, they may have had conversations I do not know about, but I felt their love and support immediately. They even offered to care for the baby so I could still go away to college if I wanted to. If you looked up unconditional love in the dictionary, you would see a picture of my parents. There was no way that I could ever leave my daughter, but they wanted to give me every opportunity for a successful life and future.

We can make plans, and then unexpected life events change the course and direction of our lives. This was one of those events that not only changed my life, I truly believe it saved my life. I was still able to graduate from high school with honors and was managing a little pretzel shop at our local mall. I was working hard to earn as much money as I possibly could before the arrival of my daughter. At the ripe age of 17, I became engaged and thought things were going in a positive direction. Even though he would come to my work and stand at the counter making sure I did not talk to anyone of the opposite sex, I did not realize the control and manipulation that was occurring. Thinking back, if I had just told my parents what was going on, I know they would have done everything they could to get me out of the situation. It could best be described as living a double life. One moment I was begging him to stop using, and the next moment I was driving back to the ATM to take out another two hundred dollars because he had to have more drugs, or he owed his dealer. All the while I was putting on a smile for my parents, convincing them that I was ready to get married.

I knew that his addiction was serious, but after another binge lasting several days and stooping to new lows, even for him, something had to give. Eventually, through ultimatums, he went to an inpatient rehab center. I made the choice (for the first of many times) to stop trying to save him and to refocus my efforts towards finally taking care of the precious life that was growing inside of me and myself. Once he was out of rehab, I regressed and convinced my parents to let him move in with us. My dad gave him a car, and we were working to prepare for our baby girl. He went to work in a construction type job and was making decent money. We went to Lamaze classes and tried to focus on preparation for our daughter who would be arriving soon. It did not take long for him to fall into old patterns and back into the drug world. There were many nights I spent looking for him, and always finding him at the wrong places. Each time I was looking, there was still part of me that hoped that time would be different, but it never was.

My beautiful gift from God, Ashley, arrived and there was still a glimmer of hope that I was clinging to that he would be able to beat his addiction. His parents were absolutely wonderful and did everything they possibly could to help him. They loved Ashley and me and wanted nothing but the best for all of us. Without going into much detail, there were multiple arrests, including in front of my parents' home several times, and so many situations that were not safe for me. The final straw was when I was at his parents' house with our daughter. We had been having a wonderful time playing with Ashley and waiting on him to get home. When he finally got home from work, which ended up being a lie because he had been fired the day before, and he stumbled in the door and was high and drunk. His dad confronted him, and in a moment of rage, he grabbed Ashley and locked himself in the room with her. His Dad was able to kick the door in and take her from him, and I took her and ran to my car. I was driving back to my parents' house, and he was quickly following me. In an effort to stop me, he rammed my Honda Accord with his truck several times as I was driving down the road. Thankfully, I had just gotten my first cell phone and called 911 as I was driving. They advised me to not stop until they arrived at my house. I not only feared for my life, I also feared for my daughter's life. After quite a struggle with the police, he was arrested… again.

Blink.
Everything changed in an instant.

This was the day that will forever be etched into my mind and is still the cause of sleepless nights and flashbacks. Trying to figure everything out on my own could have cost my daughter and me our lives. His actions that day led to my breaking point and the realization that no matter what choices he made, I would no longer let my daughter's safety be at risk. After the police took him away, I sat down with my parents and broke down. I told them about his addiction, some of the things that had been going on, and that

I thought I could save him. When I looked up, expecting to see disappointment, I saw love. They wrapped me in their arms and just let me cry. The facade no longer had to be maintained. This began the transition to the next phase of my life I refer to as the young mother phase. The wedding was off, and I was then a single mother.

Let me explain what I mean by a single mother. There are many women, of all ages who do it completely alone. When I say I was a single mother, I do not mean it in the doing everything all on my own single mother way. I was a mother, young and not with the father of my daughter, living at my amazing parents' home rent-free, and they filled in the financial, emotional, material, and maturity gaps that I lacked. It was only with the help of my parents that I was able to work to provide what I could and attend a local community college. Also, for a while, his mother graciously cared for my daughter while I was at work.

My sister was away at college and would soon be planning her wedding. My ex continued his drug use, and his addiction had taken over. He had several more inpatient rehab attempts, but the grip of addiction was too strong and he was not able to break free. He found himself in a position where he was out of money, out of drugs, and desperate for more. Later on, he told me that his addiction had gotten so far out of his control, there was not much he wouldn't do for money or drugs. Thus, through a series of bad decisions, he ended up in jail for three years.

It was around this same time my dad was diagnosed with lung and brain cancer and soon retired from his long career with the postal service. I began a new job as a 911 dispatcher and worked days, nights, and overnight shifts. My parents and I decided that a daily preschool at the home of a dear woman from our church would be best for our little girl. My beloved dad fought hard and endured chemo and radiation in an effort to give him a little more time. By the time the cancer was found, it was stage IV and inoperable. No matter how badly he felt, I do not ever remember a time where he did not light up with sheer joy the moment he saw Ashley. His day would begin by taking her to preschool, and he would come home and rest until it was time to go pick her up.

The hard decision to stop treatment was made, and my mother would soon retire from her career as the director of the local chapter of the Red Cross. She took excellent care of him and never complained, no matter how hard it was. In good times and bad. In sickness and in health. For better or for worse. She stuck by those words and advocated for him to ensure he was getting the best possible care.

Grit. That is the only way I can describe the long and courageous fight he put up against cancer. My dad managed to walk my sister down the aisle for her August wedding and even danced with her for the father/daughter dance. He was not able to speak much, so he had his best friend deliver a speech. While my sister is no longer married to her first husband, I like to think of her wedding as a final celebration of dad's life, with him here. He passed away the following month, the day after my twenty-second birthday.

It was after his death, the day after actually, that I began working a second job as a 911 dispatcher for a different city. Things were going fairly well, adjusting to our new normal without my dad. I purchased a townhouse, and my daughter and I moved about two miles from my mom. While I was so determined to be independent, there was no way that I would now consider myself independent back then. Oh, what I put my poor mom through.

The time was nearing that my ex would be getting released, and I was more and more nervous about what my life would be like. His relentless letters became more and more troublesome with threats of taking my daughter and me never seeing her again. Arriving home, after working an overnight shift, my front door was open and my townhouse had been searched. The only thing touched were the letters from my ex. He never admitted to having someone break in, but it left me uneasy, and the need to put protective measures in place for Ashley and myself became a top priority. This led to me (with the help of my super mom) selling my townhouse, quitting my jobs, and moving over two hours away. I began a new career in insurance and starting over was as refreshing as it was terrifying.

While our time away was an adventure, my ex's time out of jail was short-lived and only lasted seven months, he has been in prison since 2003. Once I knew that I no longer had to fear for my safety with him back in prison, it was time for me to come home… again. Ashley and I moved back into my mom's house. I was dating and going out more than ever because my mom was home and available. Thinking back, I missed out on precious time with my daughter and left my mother with the majority of the responsibility of raising her for several years. No matter what, my mom was there, for me and for Ashley.

Many times I have looked back with sadness, thinking about all the things that I did wrong. Carrying around that guilt and shame did not do any good, and through prayer and asking forgiveness from God and from my daughter, I no longer have that baggage. I did the best I could, and that is all anyone can do. Ashley was my gift from God, sent to save me. He trusted me with this life. He chose me to be her mother, and even though He knew I would make mistakes, He knew that I would love her with every part of my being and vow to do my part to care for and protect her, at any cost. The twists and turns and more life experience than many have in a lifetime are what helped transform me from the young naïve girl to the well -rounded woman with a passion to help others, especially single mothers. God can take every mistake, every wrong turn, and what feels like every failure and transform it into a masterpiece, a new path, and a victory.

CHAPTER 3

From Karaoke to Colorado

God's timing is always perfect, even when we don't understand it. Every time I thought I had things figured out, He showed me how much I didn't know and needed to just trust Him. I spent a long time running from one failed relationship to the next, staying in relationships I knew were not right, just because it was more fun to be with someone than to be alone. It sounds ridiculous, and it probably was, but I think that this is probably the norm more than the exception these days. We find ourselves not wanting to be alone, so we settle by staying in that relationship just a little too long, we make one more excuse as to how they can change if I just...

Change is a funny thing. There are many times that I have been so focused on changing someone else that I miss what God is trying to show me about where and what I, myself, need to work on and change. The change could mean it was the end of the relationship, but instead of listening to that knowing push from Holy Spirit, I continued on, determined to rescue someone who did not want rescuing. How pompous of me to think that me, little me, can change someone to fit my desires and needs. The reality is that I could have saved myself a lot of time, effort, and hurt if I had just turned to God, asking Him what I needed to learn and do in that moment.

It became almost easier for me to focus on other people's issues and hang-ups instead of looking at my own. I lost myself somewhere during this time. While I was so busy feeling like I was saving the world one person at a time, my self-worth and value were diminishing because it was not possible, in my mind, for someone to love me just for me. This is a dangerous place to be, and this line of thinking led to one bad decision after another. When all I could see was the fault, failures, and specks in others' eyes, that huge plank in my eye became forgotten and hidden deep down.

As I was reading my Bible on one rare occasion, I turned to Matthew, and while I was studying, I got held up on Chapter 7, specifically verses 1-5 (TPT)

> "Refuse to be a critic full of bias toward others, and judgment will not be passed on you. For you'll be judged by the same standard that you've used to judge others. The measurement you use on them will be used on you. Why would you focus on the flaw in someone else's life and yet fail to notice the glaring flaws of your own? How could you say to your friend, 'Let me show you where you're wrong, 'when you're guilty of even more? You're being hypercritical and a hypocrite! First, acknowledge your own 'blind spots' and deal with them, and then you'll be capable of dealing with the 'blind spot' of your friend."

God was directing me to my own flaws, trying to get me to focus on myself, but stubbornly, my prayer that morning was "God, show me how to help others. If I can just fix them or show them their flaws..." The rest of that prayer was completely about all the messed up people in my life and did not mention anything about showing me what I needed to change or focus on. Pride? Ego? Blindness? Fear? I was good. It was everyone else that had issues. That makes me laugh just typing it out. So ridiculous. Unfortunately, I don't think it is all that uncommon. The more we focus on others and what their problems are, the less we think about our problems, and maybe, just maybe, others won't see the problems we are so desperately trying to hide.

My time spent with God and praying was becoming less and less, and my time spent going out with friends, drinking, and focusing on worldly things to meet my needs became my new normal. I got into the habit of skipping church once or twice a month, to attending only once every few months, to only attending on Easter and Christmas Eve. Ultimately this turned into me completely forgetting about going to church. I would never say that I was not a Christian, but my actions and behavior certainly did not align with someone living their life to honor God. The details of this time in my life are certainly foggy, to say the least, and having fun became my top goal. There's not much that I haven't seen, done, or been around. I don't say that in a proud way. I say it in a way to praise God for standing beside me while I was on this path of self-destruction.

I ridiculously decided that moving during this time of my life, while I was clearly all over the place and stability was lacking, would be a good choice for myself and for Ashley. At this point, I had decided that there was no such thing as "Mr. Right" and that dating for fun, without getting too attached, was the plan. One night, I decided to go to a karaoke bar with a friend to have some drinks and fun. The bar was nearly an hour away and there were many other places we could have gone that were closer, but we decided that this particular bar was going to be the spot for the night.

By the time we got there, the bar was pretty crowded. We walked around to check it out and found a spot at the bar. I noticed a group of guys, one in particular, but did not say anything to them. They clearly were a few drinks ahead of us, and I was not one to go up and just start a conversation without liquid courage to help me. After a few shots and drinks we were having a good time talking to people around us. That same guy that I noticed right away happened to be singing "Long Black Train" by Josh Turner, and I was mesmerized.

Once he finished, he came to the bar near where I was, and I decided to go strike up a conversation. Our group ended up joining their group, and we chatted for a while. The details of the night are fuzzy, but I certainly remembered him making me laugh and thinking he was really cute. The night ended, and I thought that would probably be the last I saw of him, being that we never even exchanged numbers. As I headed home, I couldn't get this guy out of my head.

I ended up going back to that same bar the next weekend because it was such a fun spot. The people were welcoming, it was a neighborhood bar, and the drinks were strong, making it a soon to be favorite hangout. My friend was with me again, and I noticed some of the same group that was there the weekend before. I decided to talk to one of the guys I recognized to see where the one who caught my eye was. Come to find out, he was in the Navy and out on a short detachment, but would be back later that week. I did find out his name, Rich, and the one I was asking for the information happened to be the roommate of the mystery man. Rich may have told me his name the previous weekend, but I had not remembered due to my level of alcohol consumption.

Growing up in a military town, a lot of people come and go, and I had never dated anyone in the military for this reason. These were the days before Facebook, Snapchat, and Instagram, and MySpace was what everyone used. The next day, I was able to do some searching and found him on MySpace. Having already confirmed that he was single, I decided to send a message to say hi and that I hoped I would see him around sometime. Never in a million years did I think that he would remember me. To my surprise, he did, and we ended up talking a little bit. He seemed like a nice guy. However, my faith in meaningful relationships was not yet restored, so the expectation was low for a favorable outcome.

After a particularly stressful day, my friend and I decided to make the drive back to the karaoke bar. It was midweek, so we were expecting a pretty empty place, and our assumption was correct.

There were few people in there, with the exception of the few regulars. I was chatting with the bartender about the problems of the day when in walked mystery man Rich with his roommate. I was a bit taken aback because he was taller and even more handsome than I remembered. They came and sat by us, and we started talking and enjoying drinks together. While my friend was singing, Rich said that he was a bit confused as to why I was messaging him when I was with someone else. I did not understand and asked him what he meant. He explained that every time he saw me, I was with a guy. The light bulb went off, and I explained to him that the guy I was with was my friend, and that it was indeed him I was interested in. It was his nervous smile, his kind nature, and his ability to go shot for shot with me that was impressive.

To this day, we both have very different versions of how we met. He remembers coming up to me and trying to talk to me, but me ignoring him. We continue to argue and poke fun with each other about how things actually went down, but of course I am right!

He left for another detachment with the Navy and was gone for three weeks. We decided that we would do our best to keep in touch while he was gone to get to know each other better. This time away was a tremendous blessing and really helped our friendship develop into a dating relationship. With the alcohol stripped away and the ability to be completely transparent with our words with the safety of a keyboard and email, our communication was not only freeing, but also enlightening. I found out that he was from Colorado and had a love of cooking, traveling, the outdoors, his family, and having a good time.

We communicated every day through email, often several times a day. As the time drew closer for his return, I was nervous because I really liked him. Just as I had sworn off relationships, this man with great potential came into my life. We decided that we would have an official date when he returned. Of course we were going to meet at the karaoke bar. I arrived, somewhat nervous, and found a spot at the bar. I decided that I would order a drink to calm my nerves as I waited. Five minutes passed. Ten minutes. Thirty minutes. I had given up after an hour and decided that I was just going to have fun since this guy stood me up. There were several people there that I knew from my frequent visits, so I was enjoying myself anyway when in he walked. Rich found me at the bar, apologized for being late. He told me that he was on the phone with his dad and that was why he was late. I am pretty sure my face aligned with my words of a sarcastic, "riiight." After giving him a hard time for a few minutes, we ended up laughing and talking the night away. As much as I didn't want to admit it, I really liked this guy.

Things progressed, and we were spending a lot of time together. Many times this involved alcohol, some conversation, and tons of bad decisions. He had many Navy friends who shared the same bachelor lifestyle. After several weeks, I decided to introduce Rich to Ashley. She had just turned nine, and we met him at the bowling alley, where he played the arcade games with her and talked about how he met Paula, who became his stepmom, when he was nine years old. He clearly understood the need to build a friendship with my daughter first and foremost. I was hesitant about introducing her to just any guy, but Rich was different.

Reflecting on our chance encounter, there is no doubt in my mind that it was not by chance at all, but a part of God's plan. Rich was from Colorado, over 1500 miles away, and the likelihood of him being stationed in Virginia Beach as opposed to the West Coast was not high, but God had a plan. On a random night, I drove one hour to a bar while passing hundreds of other locations on the way. The same bar where Rich happened to be. Not quite so random, but God had a plan. We were both broken, in stages of our lives where a relationship did not make sense, but God had a plan. I had no idea early on that God sent this man to catch my eye by singing one of his favorite songs to change my life. Was it coincidence that he picked the song he sang? I say absolutely not. Josh Turner wrote this song that perfectly described what we were going through, yet we were so wrapped up in the world and our demons that we did not see. In case you have never heard the song or listened to the lyrics, it is important to see how God was working: "There's a long black train coming down the line, feeding off the souls that are lost and crying. Look to the heavens...you can find redemption...'cause there's victory in The Lord I say. Cling to the Father and His holy name and don't go riding on that long black train..."

We were both passengers on separate black trains, going in the wrong direction, away from the Lord. Neither of us were strong enough, in our eyes at the time, to step off that train alone, and it would take each other, in our lowest times, holding hands and jumping off that train together. But we weren't exactly ready to let go so easily. The train was comfortable, and we had gotten used to our seats on board, if you will.

Often, I would stay at his apartment instead of making the drive back home an hour away. The routine of staying there quickly became more frequent, and I rarely went back to my house. Ashley would stay with me or spend the night at my mother's house. We found ourselves drinking more and more and had names like "Messy Monday," "Tequila Tuesday," "Wine Wednesday," "Thirsty Thursday," "Fireball Friday," and "Sloppy Saturday." You get the idea. Our relationship was building, but on a foundation of liquid, which is certainly not firm or steady.

I went to the doctor for a routine annual check-up and time stood still, it seemed, when she walked in the room and said, "Congratulations! You're pregnant!"

Blink.
Blink.
Blink.

CHAPTER 4

Life and Loss

There I sat in the Target parking lot, because where else would one go after finding out they are pregnant, in a newish relationship, while in a stage of life that was really not prepared for a child? I wandered around the aisles, aimlessly searching for nothing, while a million thoughts went through my mind. Why now? What am I going to do? Is he going to stay? Am I going to have to do this alone, again? How am I going to tell him? How am I going to tell my mom? I somehow managed to pick out a baby toy, a "Welcome Baby" card, and a cute baby outfit to wrap up to give to Rich, along with the pregnancy test. Yes, I put the test in there, but I at least had the wherewithal to put it in an enclosed bag! I made it back to the car and decided I needed to call someone to process this. So, I called my aunt in Florida. She congratulated me and assured me of all the things I needed to hear, and I decided to go share the news with Rich.

He had duty the night before, which means he had to stay at the naval base overnight, and he was sleeping when I got to his apartment. I decided to put the gift bag beside him and wait for him to wake up. That lasted about one minute, and I couldn't take the waiting, so I woke him up, and told him I had a surprise for him. He opened the card, read it with a confused look, and started pulling things out of the bag. He pulled out the baby rattle, the onesie, and finally the pregnancy test. I am pretty sure that is when it all clicked. He was very excited, and we chatted away about all of the events of the day and the complete shock and blessing this was. I scheduled another appointment with my midwife because I really had no idea how far along I was, and then I had immediate guilt thinking about how I treated my body and how much alcohol I had consumed while this tiny life was growing.

Rich proposed to me on Easter and then asked permission from Ashley to marry me, which of course she was thrilled about. We shared our engagement news with his mom and dad that morning and then with my family at our family gathering later in the day. Life was moving in a positive direction, and I was excited about the future. I had a good job as a contractor at the local shipyard, Rich was nearing the end of his enlistment period with plans to work as a contractor doing the same type of work, and our relationship was good.

I started having some symptoms that were a bit concerning, so I went to my midwife and she confirmed what I had feared. She told me, with tears in her eyes, that we had lost the baby. She explained what would happen in the near future and the warning signs that I may need to go to the hospital. We were absolutely devastated that this blessing was gone as fast as it was given. In addition to the grief of the loss, I also blamed myself for the loss. If I had not been drinking, if I had gotten more rest, if I had not done such terrible things in my past, then I wouldn't have been punished for my behavior. Why would God allow this to happen? I was so angry with God. I was angry with Him, but even angrier with myself.

That night, Rich laid with me as we mourned the loss of our baby. I went to the bathroom and knew that something was not right. I was hemorrhaging and knew that this was the main warning sign that I was told about that would require medical attention. I called my mom, who was graciously caring for my daughter, to let her know what was going on, and we went to the emergency room. By the time we got there, I had lost so much blood that I could not stand, and they took me to the back right away. Much of what happened next I do not remember, but I do remember that Rich never left my side and was extremely worried about me. After several procedures, IVs, transfusions, and endless tears, we were able to go home.

My mom was so worried and wanted me to come to her house, but when I told her that Rich was taking excellent care of me and that I wanted to stay with him, she knew that he was the one for me. In the past, any time I have had major medical concerns, there's no one else that I wanted, but my mama. There is just something special about your mom taking care of you when you are sick. Somehow, she always knew when I needed something, was hurting, or just needed her comforting presence. When I found that with Rich, something shifted in my thinking. He genuinely cared about my wellbeing, he hurt because I was hurting, and he advocated for me when I could not do it for myself.

As we tended to my needs at home, we started talking about God. If there was a God, which we both knew there was, then how in the world could He let this happen? We were angry. We were sad. We didn't understand.

We.

For the first time I had experienced tragedy, and there was still a "we," not just an "I," picking up the pieces. In my mind, there would be no reason for him to have to stay now that we had lost the baby. I had braced myself for not only losing the baby, but also for losing him as well. In my past experiences, men have always left when things get hard. Did I see God the same way as I was seeing men? Was I afraid to fully surrender to Him out of fear of rejection or disappointment? Unfortunately, the answer is yes. Living my life, saying I was a Christian, while being careless and reckless somehow felt safer than fully trusting God.

For years, I carried around a deep, dark secret that I never spoke about. I was too ashamed, it was too bad, and if I told anyone, then they would never think of me the same way. This had to be the cause of the tragic miscarriage we were dealing with. It was my fault. How could I ever tell Rich that it was my actions of the past that caused this to happen? Could I possibly risk losing him by telling him what I had done? Not yet.

This could go in many different directions, and I just was not sure what that looked like in that moment. We could grow closer, end things, run away from God together, or run towards God through this loss. I was so broken and hurt that I just did not know, still trying to somehow control the outcome without trusting God.

As we turned to one another during this time of grief and mourning, we began to have more conversations about God. We had basically barricaded ourselves in his apartment and found comfort in one another. Rich shared with me that one night, when he was a young teenager; he went upstairs after not being able to fall asleep at his dad's house. He found his stepmom, Paula, reading her Bible, and she invited him to sit with her. When Rich opened his Bible, he turned to Ecclesiastes 3:1-8, Holy Spirit washed over him, and he knew that God was speaking to him in that moment. It was his time.

A Time for Everything

> "There is a time for everything and a season for every activity under the heavens: a time to be born and a time to die, a time to plant and a time to uproot, a time to kill and a time to heal, a time to tear down and a time to build, a time to weep and a time to laugh, a time to mourn and a time to dance, a time to scatter stones and a time to gather them, a time to embrace and a time to refrain from embracing, a time to search and a time to give up, a time to keep and a time to throw away, a time to tear and a time to mend, a time to be silent and a time to speak, a time to love and a time to hate, a time for war and a time for peace." Ecclesiastes 3:1-8 (NIV)

We talked about how good God has been to us in our lives, even while we were both running as fast as we could in what would seemingly be the wrong direction, and how He brought us together through a chance encounter, which can only be explained as God's perfect plan. We knew that His timing is always right because if we had met at any other time of our lives up to that point, it would not have worked. We were not ready for our lives to be rocked in a way that only He could do. If I had to describe our lives when our worlds collided, it would be hurting, broken, addicted, lost, searching, resisting, and certainly not looking for a relationship.

God is a loving God, and He does not retaliate against us when we sin. He just loves us and forgives us. We talked about how there is no sin greater than another, how God hurts when we hurt, and that there are things that just can't be explained on this side of heaven. Although there was no longer a life that we were going to bring into the world, we would hold our precious baby when we get to heaven. We also knew it was time to change our lifestyle and behaviors to bring Him honor. Looking back, this is what ultimately brought us closer to each other and would be what joined us together.

In order to make the changes that we talked about, there had to be some type of action plan or steps in place. My body healed, and we were working on healing emotionally. We knew that we wanted to somehow incorporate God into our lives, but we did not know what that looked like at that point. I would describe our initial revelation as us living our lives with an occasional conversation about Jesus. It was certainly not ideal, but we did know that we wanted our foundation to be built on Christ, that we had the same beliefs, and that, through this tragedy, we wanted to stay together. We talked about church and our desire to find one that we both liked, knowing what we did not want in a church, and eager to connect with other people. We talked a good game, but then Saturday night would happen, and we would be too hungover to go on Sunday morning. We stayed in this cycle of talking about church for quite a while without ever going to one. We would sometimes listen to a sermon on television if we happened to stop on the channel, but we were not ready to commit. Talk without action is just talk.

But that secret I had.

The secret still loomed. There were a handful of people that knew, and I was pretty sure that I would be able to live my life being okay with just them knowing. Those that knew, loved me, did not think poorly of me, and supported me as best they could during the process. I spent so many years pushing it down, convincing myself that I had forgotten about it, and beating myself up that mentally I was more abusive to myself than anyone else could ever possibly be to me. As long as I didn't risk exposing myself to anyone, then I could hide the hurt and pain I was holding for over ten years and remain safe in my bubble. While I knew in my heart that God was not punishing me for my actions as a teenager, in my mind I could not make those thoughts stop. They began to consume me. How could I have done that? There were so many other ways I could have handled the situation. Why did I pick the one I did?

I didn't deserve a baby. There. I said it. That is how I felt, and the only way to work through those feelings was to confess my sins to God, and to Rich.

But that was hard.

So hard.

It's one thing to keep it inside; it's a completely other level to be fully transparent and vulnerable with another person, exposing the very part of you that you hate. Was this the time? I just did not know. I had to determine if my faith in God, in Rich, and in myself was bigger than ten years' worth of mental abuse I held so tightly to and bigger than all of the but's that kept me from speaking the words.

God's plans and ways are just so perfect. The same verse that Rich was reading when he was baptized in the Holy Spirit set me free from years of pain. Ecclesiastes 3:7 (NASB) says "A time to tear apart and a time to sew together; A time to be silent and a time to speak." We could either be torn apart and our relationship end because of my secret, or sewn together through confession of my secret. Was this the time to be silent, or the time to speak? I just didn't know.

This verse is so much more than a simple reference of time for me. It is a representation of the vulnerable stages of my heart. In order for my heart to heal from where it had been torn apart, I had to speak up. It could only be sewn together after breaking the silence. God is the ultimate seamstress, weaving the tapestry of life into His beautiful masterpiece. Each piece of my life fits together and has formed me into the woman I am today. No matter how many stains are on it, He washes it clean. Because His love is so powerful, there is no stain too great for His removal.

So why did I think that my sin was above God's power of forgiveness? It was time to surrender and begin the healing process that I was running from. He parts the seas, can move mountains, and breathed life into our lungs, but I did not believe He could forgive me until I was ready to accept that forgiveness.

It was time.

We sat in the parking lot of a restaurant and decided to let our walls down, deciding that if we were going to make this work, there could be no secrets and we would need to have transparency. He shared with me his secrets, and then it was my turn. There was no turning back. I took a deep breath and decided that it was time to trust and that no matter what happened, I was going to be okay.

Here goes nothing.

Nervous eyes. Blink.
Tear-filled eyes. Blink.
Freedom-found eyes. Blink.

CHAPTER 5

Freedom in Surrendering

Our minds can certainly be our best friends and worst enemies all at once. I had built up, for ten years, that I was the worst person in the world, only to find out Rich kept secrets that he felt the same way about in his mind. After he shared with me his, which I will not spill here nor anywhere, my response was, "that's it?"! Of course there was more conversation, but in that moment, the years of guilt, shame, anger, and hurt were all erased, and the relief and peace that came from sharing with God, through speaking to me and confessing his sins, overcame him. It was like he was a new man. In that moment, I witnessed the almighty power of God and the healing that can be given just by asking for it. I wanted that for myself so badly.

Did I have to go through someone else to find forgiveness with God? No, God could forgive me by me going directly to Him and asking for it. It is when we confess our sins to others and we come together in prayer that powerful healing can occur. In James 5:16, "Therefore confess your sins to each other and pray for each other so that you may be healed. The prayer of a righteous person is powerful and effective." My interpretation is that God wants us to share not only our good moments, but also the not so good, happy, exciting, hurtful, life, death, mourning, celebrating, and all the ups and downs we face in life with others. His desire is for us to live in a community where we feel safe, can hold each other accountable, and pray for one another.

I think about how Jesus lived, the community he built around Him, and how He spent time with those He trusted. Like the relationships of today, there was betrayal, hurt, sadness, and failures, but there was also loyalty, friendship, miracles, and so many lessons shared. I am certainly not suggesting that we should go around telling all of our secrets to everyone we meet, but having relationships that are genuine and trustworthy are so necessary. I think this was part of what I was missing for so long in my life. This could also help explain the years of protective layers that I had carefully constructed around myself, keeping it all in.

After a while, the layers had become so heavy that it was like walking around with a full suit of armor. This type of armor is nothing like the armor of God. It is feeling like each step is a little heavier than the last. It is never being real with anyone because the protective layer is just too thick to penetrate and actually get through. It is very lonely and heavy. So heavy that there were days that the weight felt too much to carry and thoughts about just ending things would be the only answer. Secrets and fear of what others think is not a great place to live, and it is where your true identity disappears.

It was my turn to start talking. Sitting there in my seat of the car, I felt such heaviness while Rich was free from his years of secrets and pain. Could it simply be that easy? I was about to find out.

Deep breath. Blink.
What if? Blink.
God give me strength. Blink.

Remember when I told you I was 18 years old and I had an infant and a boyfriend who was an addict in and out of jail? Remember I was living with my parents because there was absolutely no way that I could support myself and my child, and I was working a minimum wage job? Remember I had aspirations of attending college and had begun taking courses at the local community college? That was about the same time when my dad came home one day and said I was acting moody. I laugh now because what 18-year-old isn't moody? I didn't think anything of it because I was already dealing with more than I thought I could handle. He asked me if I could be pregnant again, and I laughed and said no way. My mom gave him a look, and one of them went out to get a test for me to take.

The next few days seem like a blur, and I do not know how I could have gotten through it without the love and support of my mom. I begrudgingly took the test because I knew that there was no way possible it would be positive. It just couldn't be.

I remember being in the bathroom of my parents' bedroom and my world stopping. It was one of those moments where sound disappears, things move in slow motion, and my heartbeat was as loud as a drum. I couldn't breathe. I couldn't move. I couldn't stop the tears that began instantly and quickly turned into sobs. There was no question. The bright plus sign showed immediately. I was pregnant. Again.

Things could have been worse. I could have been alone, but the moment I had the courage to open the bathroom door, my mom was standing there, tears falling from her eyes, waiting to embrace me, in the way only a mother could when her baby was hurting. She let me fall apart in her arms as my dad stood there offering his support. I began sobbing again, repeating over and over, "I can't do this. I can't do this."

I was single, barely raising a baby, and the same father that was absent for my first child would certainly be absent for the second. My parents were doing the best they could to help support me, my daughter, my grandfather and grandmother, who also lived with us, and my sister, who was away at college. There was no extra money. There was no more space. There was no help from any organization because I lived with parents who were employed, and my minimum wage job put me over the income level. The advice given to me when

I applied for some type of help was to quit my job and then come back and apply. I did qualify for the Special Supplemental Nutrition Program for Women, Infants, and Children (WIC), which provided formula and some food items, and I was very grateful for that. The other expenses, such as diapers, clothes, wipes, tuition, childcare, insurance, groceries and gas, took all of my paycheck. I didn't even have to pay rent to my parents, which is the only reason I was not homeless with Ashley.

Now I had to consider another child? I knew in that moment that I had a choice to make. A choice that I never, not in a million years, thought that I would have to make. I did not give myself time to process all of my options, I just knew that there was a sense of urgency in my mind. Once the decision was made, I would not change my mind. But how does one make that kind of decision? How do you decide if you let your child live or end its life? How do you consider a choice that you do not believe in?

I could hear them then, and I can hear them now: the comments from well-meaning people, words that cut so deeply to the core that it feels like it could be the reason I am anemic. Words spoken in a group setting from those, never having been in the situation themselves, declaring how God could never forgive someone for murdering their baby; voices of "there are other options," and "how could anyone even consider it if you are a Christian?" and "they made the choice to have sex, now they have to face the consequences!" and "there are plenty of people who want a child that can't have one!" and "there are programs out there to help," and finally, "you can't possibly be forgiven if you have done that." These voices and opinions are so loud, that the quiet, shaky voices of those wanting so desperately to say "me too" are muted. There is a feeling that if you ever so much as mention it, people will never look at you the same. You become "one of those people."

I wish I could share with you the story of the outpouring of help, other than from family, that I received when I was 18, single and raising a newborn, but that just is not true. I got whispers behind my back, obvious glares of disapproval, and more feelings of shame and unworthiness than anyone should ever have to feel. Sadly, most of these instances, and there were many, occurred from those who were Christians or from inside the walls of a church. Are we standing so firmly in what we believe is right and wrong that we fail to remember to love and support? Are we so worried about the events that caused one to be fatherless or orphans that we fail to step in to help as God calls us to do?

In a world of such hard, fast judgment, what if we took the time to slow down and listen. Imagine the difference an entire generation could make if we just love one another and shared each other's burdens. Instead of throwing out a quick "I'll pray for you," you show up and pray for them, bring a meal to someone who is having a hard time financially, or rake the leaves of the widow next door, without expecting anything in return. What if we take time to show our children what it means to serve others and put someone else's needs ahead of our own? It just takes a little effort and a lot of love.

As I sat on my parents' bed, being held by my mom, the decision was made that night. The next morning, we called and got an appointment at the clinic for the following day. Three days. That is the length of time that I had, well once I found out about it, with this little life. That number three again. There is such significance with that number for me. I had come to terms with the fact that I would not be having a second child. Once the decision was made, in my mind I believed that I would not have to think about it anymore, and it would just be erased from my memory. I was very wrong. There has not been a day that has gone by that I do not think about it.

My mom drove me to the clinic, sitting beside me, providing as much support as she possibly could. I think at that time it was harder for her than it was for me. She knew the pain I was in, and there was nothing she could do to take it away. As a mother, that pain is indescribable. Walking in, there were protestors lining the sidewalk, baring posters of mutilated babies and words like "killer" and "sinner," all while screaming into a megaphone about how we were going to hell.

We made it inside, through the wave of people and their attempts to block the door, and waited for them to call me back. It seemed like hours before I went into that cold, sterile room alone. The first step was to start an IV. Four tries later, that was in and they had me lay down for an ultrasound. The words she said will forever be etched into my mind. "Oh wow! There's two in there! You're getting a good two for one deal today." What? It took me a moment to realize what she meant; I was pregnant with twins. I asked if I could please have a copy of the ultrasound, some tangible item to remember my babies with. She said no, they don't print them and that it was just a guide to make sure the pregnancy was where it was supposed to be in the uterus.

I wanted my mom.
I wanted to leave.
I wanted it to be a nightmare.
But it wasn't.
Blink.

It was in that moment that I begged God to take my babies, for them to be with Him, and for it to be as painful as possible so that I would never forget that moment. When we got to the car, I looked over at my mom and told her there were two babies, and we hugged and cried together. There are no words that can describe the pain felt in that moment and the hole that remains in my heart.

My sister and aunt were at our house when we got there, and their love and support, in a time that I had no love for myself, helped ease the pain of the next few days. Slowly, life began to return to normal. The physical pain subsided. The mental pain was pushed way down, so deep that it would stay there for the next almost ten years. There were many times that the "what ifs" and "if I had only" nearly took over my mind. What if I had taken a different path? If only I had carried them to term and given them up for adoption. If I could go back and make the decision again, would I change the outcome? The almost 40-year-old version of me says absolutely, but I feel the 18-year-old version of me did the best she could. People ask, if you could go back in time and change one thing, what would it be? I always come back to this day, this decision, and the loss of these lives. Letting myself stay in this loop of unhealthy, repetitive mental torture would and could not change the past, but it could help change the future for someone else.

Sitting in the car with Rich, sharing this painful, horrible, unimaginable secret that was kept for nearly a decade, I was unable to make eye contact because I knew he would be judging me and ready to drop me off. Only, when I had the courage to finally look up, through my tears, I saw tears in his eyes. He wiped the tears off my cheek, told me how awful that must have been to keep inside for so long, and thanked me for trusting him enough to share it with him. He told me how much he loved me and how this certainly did not change how he felt about me, and he just held me.

For both of us, it took sharing our past hurts and deep pains, finding true transparency with one another, that we were able to ask forgiveness from God. All of the years of carrying the unforgiveness and shame were unnecessary. God forgave us instantly in that moment. It would take much longer for each of us to learn how to forgive ourselves. I told him that I felt like we lost our baby because of my actions and that I had tremendous guilt because it was my fault. The words he spoke to me in that moment changed everything. He said that our God is a loving God, one who hurts when we hurt. God is there to wipe our tears and to carry us when our burdens are too heavy. He said that we are all sinners, which is why He sent Jesus Christ to save us. Jesus felt the hurts, loss, and betrayal, as well as joy, laughter, and loyalty. God understands our pain and is the one who can take it away through forgiveness of our sin. He can take it away. My deeply hidden, hard to even speak, ugliest, worst of the worst sin can be forgiven. There is nothing too hard, bad, or great of a sin that God can't handle. Did I think that I was above God? My gut reaction was, "of course not!" Then why did I think that when He tells us to go to Him and confess our sins that my sin was greater than what He can forgive?

Shortly after this relationship-defining conversation, I started to plan a surprise for Rich's birthday. I had shared with him the worst parts of my life and I wanted to share with him some of the best parts. I love planning a good surprise, and knowing that I would be able to pull it off was exciting. No matter how big or small, Rich loves to be surprised, and I thought up the perfect idea.

CHAPTER 6

Outer Banks to the Rocky Mountains

For Rich's thirtieth birthday, I decided to surprise him with a day trip to the Outer Banks, North Carolina. We went parasailing and then further down to the Cape Hatteras Lighthouse to explore. Upon our arrival, he asked me how I knew. I really did not know what he was talking about, and he asked again how I knew that he always loved this lighthouse. I explained that the Outer Banks was a part of my childhood and adulthood and there is just something special about it that I wanted to share with him. He told me that in his room growing up at his dad's house, he had a poster of the Cape Hatteras Lighthouse, but did not know where it was. He said he had always been drawn to the water, probably indicative of him joining the Navy, and that the lighthouse was symbolic for him for many reasons. God was at work many years ago sewing this relationship together, piece by piece. The Outer Banks and North Carolina became a favorite for him as well, and we spend much time there.

As time went on, the excitement and planning for our wedding became the topic of most of our conversations. Rich and I made the decision to have our wedding and reception in Colorado so that his parents, siblings, and family could attend. In an effort to make sure that we could celebrate our union with as many of our family and friends as we could, we would have a second reception near our home in Virginia for those who were unable to travel to Colorado.

I have always been somewhat of a free spirit, go with the flow, up for an adventure type of person. The idea of planning a wedding across the country, using the internet to research everything, all while meeting my future in-laws, sisters-in-law, and nieces for the first time brought us all closer together. After talking with his family, I had confidence in selecting a venue that would be perfect. Food vendors were selected with meals that were delicious. My mother was able to help me plan while we worked with my future mother-in-law in tying down the details, including a horse-drawn carriage ride. Rich, mom, and I worked together picking out the invitations, napkins, flowers, cakes, and a location for the local reception, as well as all of the other details that come with planning a wedding and two receptions.

As if this were not enough to consider at one time, both of our leases were ending soon, and we had to make a decision about where to live. We purchased our first home in May of 2009 on a quiet, private road with a white picket fence, and a perfect size of two bedrooms and one-and-a-half bath. We were a family of three, and purchasing this home signified the solid foundation that we would start our journey, our life together.

Shortly before our wedding, Rich and I found out that we would soon become a family of four. We shared the exciting news with Ashley, my mom, and my sister and decided that we would surprise his family in person when we arrived in Colorado. We shared the news with his mom and dad and stepmom by giving them a card with the news and watching their faces light up. His sisters were thrilled as well, and being together, sharing that joy, is something that really meant so much to me. The Navy had taken him far away from his family for so long, that sharing exciting news in person was really special for Rich.

The wedding was beautiful as we were joined by his family all the way from Florida to Illinois and my mom, my sister and her family, my aunt and uncle, my longest friend and former neighbor who I consider my other sister and her family, and Ashley standing beside me as my maid of honor. During our ceremony, Rich not only made vows to me, but he also made vows to Ashley. He promised to love her as his daughter, to provide and care for her, and to step into the role of her dad. I was able to hold it together up until this point. To find a man who would love me is one thing; to find a man who would choose to step up and fill the role that Ashley had been praying for all of her life was another.

Once back in Virginia, we were joined by so many of our family and friends to show their love and support at our reception. Mom made sure that every detail was taken care of, down to the cake and creating the beautiful flowers with my aunt. It was truly magical for us, and we certainly felt the love and encouragement as we began married life together while anticipating the precious life that was growing beautifully.

Having family spread so far apart is hard and many compromises have had to be made, most on his side. I often take for granted the fact that I can swing by my mom's house anytime I want, while visiting his family takes much planning. I think about how much my dad would have gotten along with Rich and his dad, and I have so much sadness that they will not meet on this side of heaven. Family is precious, and the time we spend together is cherished, no matter how long we are together.

Shortly after our marriage, Rich was outside cutting back some of the overgrown bushes in the front yard. He hit an underground beehive, which would be reason to have a pest control company come out and begin treatments on our house. While they were completing their initial inspection to start, they made us aware of tremendous foundation damage and several rotten floor joists, this on a home we just purchased and did not have the means to complete the repairs. The strong foundation, without examination, had many areas of damage and concern that we were not aware of prior to purchasing. Thinking further, this not only described our home's foundation, it described our marriage and the cracks and hidden damages that we were both unintentionally hiding from one another. Our rotten boards had held us up for so long that they were just there, and it would take going deeper and really taking a hard look at what we were made of to eventually sister, or even replace, those joists with solid beams.

While I was pregnant, it became easier to notice the pattern of Rich's drinking. To say it was excessive is an understatement and, to be honest, the only reason I was not drinking with him was because I was pregnant. Our home was filled with laughter, friends, cookouts, cornhole, and, of course, drinking. Life was good, until it wasn't. Things were not always sunshine and roses in our home. There was yelling, arguing, insults, and hurtful words spoken often, usually after an evening of drinking, and when you add in pregnancy hormones, it was quite the mix.

My pregnancy was pretty easy, and I enjoyed every moment of being pregnant. I was able to work right up to delivery. In fact, I was waking up to my alarm to go in when my water broke. Rich had just gotten to work, 45 minutes away, and I decided that I should take Ashley to school. I am a pretty self-sufficient person and labor was not going to stop me from getting her to school on time. Rich got home, and we headed to the hospital. My mom barely made it to the room, and within thirty minutes of our arrival, Andrea was born. She was the light of our lives, and Ashley was so excited to finally have the sister that she had wanted for so many years.

Not long after Andrea was born, we were at a friend's house for a bonfire. She was a friend who I had known since grade school, one of the few who loved me for me, despite the mistakes of my past, she was and is always there with her genuine, caring, and loving self. Ashley was playing with other kids who were there and everyone was having a good time. Andrea was nestled in my arms, and the weather was perfect. My friend asked us to visit her church and said that she thought we would really like it. This was the first time that we had been asked to church by friends. I remember that first night she asked us very clear, but it took her asking several more times, along with the help of our other friends who attended the same church, before we decided to go. We are so thankful for her persistence.

House, check. Marriage, check. Baby, check. God, still not in the mix. We finally ran out of excuses to not go, so we decided to try it out. Everything about the experience felt like home. From the wisdom of the pastor who launched the church over twenty years before, to the music that was excellent and truly worshiped the Lord, to the friendliness of the church members, to the nursery workers who were eagerly ready for Andrea. Community. This is what a community of fellow believers felt like, and I wanted to be a part of what God had for us here. Rich and I both felt the love and acceptance there, and we decided that we wanted to continue coming back and even considered joining a small group. The idea of meeting people we did not know to talk about the Bible, share our lives with, and build relationships with was a bit intimidating. We both worried about fitting in, about maybe not knowing enough, and about sharing about our personal lives. What if they find out about our lives outside of church? I was ready to at least see what it would be like, but decided I would not share anything too personal. That outer shell of protection is hard to crack and not just everyone gets in.

We continued to go to church every Sunday. I am not sure that I would have believed anyone if they had shared that small group would be something that we would start to look forward to each week. It did not take very long for some of that tough outer cover to soften and for the members of the group to not just be acquaintances, but to become our friends. We quickly found ourselves surrounded with some of the most caring, loving, and real people that we got to go through life with. To this day, many of the members of this first group are some of my dearest friends who are like family.

Shortly after Andrea was born, four months to be exact, we found out that we were expecting again. Our two-bedroom home was getting a bit smaller than what we had anticipated needing. We were regularly attending church, but there was that lingering alcohol issue. Once pregnant, it no longer became an issue for me. After all of my past experiences and wanting to fix people and their problems, including Rich's drinking, this time was different. I knew that if I attempted to make him stop drinking, then it would backfire. I did not know what to do, so I tried something different. I prayed. Lord, help him. Lord, help me to know how to help him. Lord, only you can remove his ten-plus years of battling alcoholism. Yet, I did not see any immediate results. I was praying for him, but he was not ready. I remained silent in prayer because I knew that God heard me. For me, it also became an internal struggle of not being upset with him for not stopping just because I did, knowing I only stopped because I was pregnant. This was something that had been there when we met and I had previously been fine with this for our entire relationship.

Our church announced that there would be a corporate twenty-one-day fast. This concept was something totally foreign to me, and I had no idea what that even meant. The pastor explained that the fast did not have to be food-related, but for us to select something to fast and replace the time spent thinking about or doing whatever it was in prayer. Well, I was pregnant so that created many reasons why I could not fast food. Honestly, I do not know what I fasted during this time because it was so much bigger than what I could have ever imagined. During the first few days of the fast, Rich decided to fast from beer, leaving wine and liquor as options. Two days later, he decided to fast from beer and liquor, leaving wine as an option. Three days later, he decided to completely fast from all alcohol.

Blink.

Three days. It was three days later when he prayed for God to remove the desire for alcohol and for there to be no ill side effects from his abrupt ending to years of drinking large amounts. He prayed for the strength to never let his children see him losing his battle with alcoholism. God answered his prayer. God heard my pleading prayers. During those twenty-one days, God completely transformed Rich from the inside out, and the weight and chains that addiction had over his life had been removed. He did not have so much as a headache, and the fear of passing this behavior to his children was no longer a concern. This was the first of many miracles and answered prayers that God has shown us. The difference this time was that we relied on Him completely. It required giving up the control in a situation that in reality I had no control over anyway and turning it over to God. It took us praying, trusting, believing, pleading, and being obedient to a situation that had taken over. Never stop believing that God hears your prayers. He does.

Chapter 7

Free

There is a difference in being the person that God has set free and being married to the person that God freed. I spent many years of my teen and young adult life not being able to trust pretty much anyone other than my family. Before I met Rich, there were many nights I laid awake at night, wondering what tragedy was going to happen next. There were years that I lived with a painful uncertainty of waiting, just waiting for the next hurt because I knew it was coming. Unfortunately, I brought all of this baggage into my relationship with Rich, and the years of repeated patterns and cycles made those bags extremely heavy. Yet, I refused to let them go. For me, learning to trust his recovery did not happen overnight. Any time we would disagree or argue, I would think that he would relapse and go somewhere to drink. I remember after having a heated disagreement one night, though I do not remember what the disagreement was about, Rich left.

My mind immediately went to thoughts of him going to a bar or going to get alcohol somewhere instead of being home. I created the relapse story and drunken outcome and was ready to attack without even really knowing where he was or what he was doing. Even though I saw the miracle and the freedom that he found, I was still running behind him holding those chains of alcoholism, almost waiting to throw them back on him. I played every worst-case scenario in my mind and was so angry with him that he went right back to his old ways. He was gone for less than thirty minutes, and it took less than thirty minutes to remove all of the faith and trust that I had in him. The work that he and God were doing meant nothing in that moment, and the thought that he was stronger than the addiction had me doubting that the miracle really happened. I was prepared and had my mental list of wrongs ready to verbally attack him the moment that he returned.

He didn't return home right away, but he called me. I was not prepared for that. He was calling to let me know that he was okay and that he just needed some space to clear his head. He said that in order to not say things he didn't mean to say and to stop the continued arguing, he took a moment to drive down to the end of the street to pray. He apologized and asked if we needed anything from the store before he came home. We ended the call, and I was mad at him for not falling back into old patterns, not because he was sober, but because I was wrong.

Well, that's just great, I thought. I was ready to unload this built up anger and aggression for him relapsing, only to find out that he didn't do anything wrong. He prayed. He removed himself from the situation, took time to process what was going on, and went to His Father for guidance.

I wanted to be angry. I wanted to yell. I wanted to unleash the fantastic one-liners that I had been prepping for him. I was not prepared to not be angry. I had been conditioned to believe the worst in others, even my husband in whom I had witnessed a miracle. My first response was to protect myself, almost like a turtle retreating to hide in its hard shell like my impenetrable armor, guarding my heart and mind from more pain and suffering. Had I not learned anything? Why was his first response to go and pray, yet mine was anger and retaliation? Why did I somehow get upset that he had not failed?

There it was again: control and my pattern of thinking that I could save others from themselves. For most of my life, I thought

I was in control of situations, people, outcomes, and reactions and that if I just held on tight enough or force my way enough, then everything would be okay. I was addicted to fixing other people, thinking it was through my doing all along. Was I really taking credit for work that only God can do? Was I obsessed with enabling others so that I could be the hero in the story? Ouch.

Control is a funny thing, seemingly so apparent, yet an illusion that does not exist in the first place. I could trust God with many things, but there was no way I would surrender control of my family, or my money. This false belief that I had control over someone else's actions, thoughts, and behaviors was simply ludicrous, yet I was determined to hold on as tightly as I could. The reality is that God is in control, but I, of course, felt the need to provide assistance because certainly, I knew best. Can you see my eyes rolling as you're reading?

How many times do we try to force a situation or an outcome instead of praying about it and trusting God? I can tell you that it has been my experience that God will give you the same lesson over and over again, maybe with a slight variation, until you understand what He is trying to teach you. I had this lesson many times, and if I am being completely honest, I am still working on this one, although I am much better about realizing that God is in control.

It's not something that I am proud of, but this pattern of me assuming that he was going to drink in excess did not go away as quickly as his desire to drink did. It took many times of him not going back to alcohol for me to realize that it was my issue, my hang-up, my problem that was consuming me. Addiction doesn't just affect the person with the disease. It impacts the entire family. I think that's one thing about addiction that many people fail to realize. It takes time to learn boundaries that are healthy and setting firm yes's and no's. It does not mean that you don't love someone when you set boundaries. There are times that you have to do what is best for you and your family to create healthy boundaries. Sometimes that means loving them from a distance. It is often more painful for the one setting the boundary than the one the boundary is set for. I have found that this is because we feel guilty for putting our needs ahead of someone else who is struggling with a disease. I am certainly not suggesting not trying to help someone get help. I am suggesting that you cannot make someone want help or want to change. Only God can do that.

That phrase "you teach someone how to treat you" has been so true in my life, and there comes a point where enough is enough. This was a learning process for both of us of what sobriety meant in our home. We did not know how to communicate and certainly did not know how to work through any conflict without it becoming an all-out yelling match. It was almost a contest of who could sling the worst insult towards the other. Alcohol was a crutch, a mask if you will, for handling emotions and dealing with, or not dealing with, things that life would throw at us. When alcohol was removed, we were left with these raw, real emotions and no clue what to do with them. We knew something had to change because we both had reached the enough is enough stage, yet we did not know how we wanted to be treated or should be treated.

When we got married, we did not go to any premarital counseling to talk through our wants and needs. We really had never discussed our future hopes and dreams, other than spontaneous travel. We lived in the moment and were still in the honeymoon phase of that "we never fight" false reality. I guess you can say that I have rarely done things in the order that makes sense to most people. I was living in the fairytale mindset that we could just wing it through whatever we faced. Oh, how wrong we were.

If you do not know how to communicate or resolve conflict, then you just stay in this nasty cycle of highs and lows with a few mediums in the mix. I thought I had spent my life communicating. Of course I know how to communicate. It was him with the problem. I thought if I could just make him see how right I was, then we wouldn't be arguing about the same things over and over again.

You could almost see the mental tally chart, tracking the rights and wrongs of one another. I took the trash out. Well, I did the laundry. You left your towel on the floor. Well, you didn't unload the dishwasher. Instead of looking for positives in one another, we were finding ways to point out all of the things that the other person was not doing. We were waiting for the other to meet that 50/50 role that was magically created in our minds, yet it just wasn't obtainable. It wasn't obtainable because it simply does not exist.

Ironically, during this time I was taking a college course on marital counseling while working towards my bachelor's degree. I began to see so much of our marriage and ourselves in the counselors' case studies that we were dissecting. I brought in my old wounds from previous relationships, holding him accountable for things he did not do, or even know about for that matter. He brought in years of addiction that masked his ability to feel, causing him to have little to no understanding of how to process emotions and pressure. We each had our own ways of hiding that, yet it was bubbling out more often than we could hide.

Rich disliked conflict and was typically reserved and quiet until he reached a certain point, and then it quickly escalated to a volcano erupting, spewing lava over everything in his path. I, on the other hand, did not mind conflict, and if I saw something that bothered me, I would address it (and address it and address it). I found a lot of things that bothered me to the point that I was nagging all the time. I even got on my own nerves. If there was an issue, I thought we should address it then. He would rather take a moment to think about it, pause, and then address it later. I remember one particular afternoon something happened and he had gone to our room to take a moment. Well, being the brilliant person that I was, I began knocking on the door. I tried the handle over and over, but it was locked. Then as I was knocking, I proceeded to yell through the door. I was explaining all of the reasons that I was right and that he needed to just open the door. If he would just stop being hard-headed and talk to me, we could fix things right then and there. He was quiet and silent, yet I persisted with my knocking, yelling, and presenting my case. Why I thought that this was appropriate,

I will never know. Eventually, he opened the door and the volcano erupted. Thinking back, I was acting like a woodpecker pecking at a tree, repeatedly, over and over, just pecking away.

This day was a changing point in our relationship. I certainly do not remember everything that was said, and there may have been an old dresser waiting for the bulk trash pick-up that ended up as a casualty, but I will never forget his words, "Why don't you respect me enough to give me space when I practically begged you for it?".

I was responding to him to address my needs and how I wanted to handle the situation. I did not take his needs or how he processed things into consideration, not even for a moment. The man I respected most in this world did not feel respected by me. I did not allow him to have the space he needed to work through what he needed to before we talked. He didn't go back to alcohol in the midst of the fight. He didn't leave. He simply wanted time to process his thoughts. I took that from him.

It took verbal communication of our needs for us to really start to hear each other, not just what we *thought* the other needed. Now if he says, "give me a moment," he has all the time in the world because I know that is how he processes. When he is ready, we discuss it. It is important to have that moment, but come back to the issue when the time is right. There have been times that we have moved on from a fight, after the processing has occurred, and just acted like it never happened. We just swept that little mess right under the rug as if it didn't even happen. We did learn quickly that coming back to the issue is extremely important because sweeping things under the rug only creates a lump that you have to walk around. It doesn't have to be a long, drawn-out conversation rehashing the same things over and over, just a simple check-in is enough sometimes. The more things that are left unsaid, the larger the lump under the rug becomes, and it will eventually create such a boundary that sweeping it out becomes nearly impossible.

We continued to go to our small group and soon had a solid group of friends who were able to mentor and model what a Christ-centered marriage should look like. We talked about how God should always be in the middle of our marriage, and the closer we grew to God, the closer we would grow together.

In my mind, it was me on one side, Ashley on the other, God in the middle, and Rich after the kids. Once we were married, my thinking was no longer correct, and the more I learned and read, the more I knew that Rich had to come after God. This was not very easy for me. For nine years, Ashley was first in my life. There was no way I was putting anything or anyone in front of her. When I heard God, spouse, child, everything else, I was resistant. I wrestled with this for a long time, and thinking back, there were many times that I did not honor my husband as the head of our family. Sadly, I pretty much pushed him to the back. I overruled his decisions with Ashley to the point of making him feel like he didn't matter at times. I had to be her voice. I had to make sure she would not get hurt. Control is so hard to give up.

We began to do devotions in the evening, and each of us was really growing in our walk with the Lord. We went through a course with our church about stepfamilies, and wow, God really spoke to me. How in the world could we, we as in Rich and I, become one like Genesis 2:24 says if I am blocking and pushing him away? It took time and a lot of prayer to understand this concept. If I am being honest, it made me feel guilty to put someone else ahead of my child. To me, it meant somehow loving her less, when in fact it was anything but that.

In order for our marriage to work and thrive, we had to make some major changes in our minds, hearts, and household. We were sitting in church one Sunday, and it happened to be baptism weekend. Rich had been water baptized as a teenager, and I had been "sprinkled" as a young child. The thought of walking to the front of the church, to get in a pool, and be baptized did not appeal to me. Nope, no thanks. I was good with my sprinkling.

We were worshiping and cheering for all of the people who were being baptized. I started to feel a nudge, but there was no way would

I listen. The next moments are like a scene from a movie, a period of time where every detail is chiseled in my memory. Each time I hear the beautiful song by Chris Tomlin, "Amazing Grace (My Chains are Gone)," I am brought to tears remembering this moment.

I decided that it would be important to share the battle that was happening inside of my mind because I think there may be others that have felt or feel the same way and have yet to act on those feelings.

The music began for the next song and God was speaking to me...

"...I once was lost, but now I'm found..."

My inner dialogue was battling, and I was trying to fight what was going on. What was happening? There were tears that I could not stop. My arms lifted in worship. Who was this person? It certainly was not me! I couldn't raise my hands in worship! Someone might see me! Someone might laugh! Someone might wonder what in the world I was doing.

"...How precious did that grace appear..."

Grace. Even for a sinner like me? Jesus, you've heard my cries, my pleas for forgiveness. Can you take this pain and baggage and love someone as sinful as I am? I do believe you can, Jesus.

"...My chains are gone"

These chains are so heavy. There are so many! I want to be free, but oh these chains. Unending love. I want that Jesus, but... I felt like Jesus stopped the rest of that sentence and spoke to me, "unending love, amazing grace." There is no but. There is no sin exception. There is no condition to meet. He said unending love, amazing grace.

The next thing I knew, I was moving. The battle continued inside with thoughts of, "Nope. I am not ready to do this! I am wearing my jeans. I do not have a towel, and this will be so embarrassing!" Yet, I was still moving towards the front of the church.

"...The Lord has promised good to me..."

God's promises are so good, even for a sinner like me! Do I trust enough to put my hope in His word? I want to, but it is so hard. I've done too much. I was nearly to the front of the church, jeans and all.

"…I've been set free…"

"…Unending love, amazing grace…"

Yes! I want to be free! I was in my own head and did not really pay attention to what was happening around me. All of a sudden, Rich is standing beside me, grabbing my hand, tears in his eyes. He said that he was ready to start life, fully free, forgiven, and dropping our chains in that baptismal pool. He said there was no way that I was going to do this alone and assured me that we were in this together.

Blink.

We climbed in and were baptized and, as we came out of the water, we were free.

"…But God, who called me here below…"

"…You are forever mine"

CHAPTER 8
He Said She Said

From this point forward, everything was seamless and we had it all figured out. No fighting, perfect parenting, and we were walking on sunshine! Ha! I am guessing you don't believe me either. I think that there is often the misconception that once you go all-in for Jesus and take steps to change your life, then all of your problems just dissipate. The problems are still there. How you look at the problems and where and who you turn towards to get through each obstacle is what changes.

We were a family of four, both of us working good jobs. Ashley was in upper elementary school, and things were going well. Rich knew that his sobriety and example for our children was worth more than any drink, and he openly and willingly shared his struggle with alcohol and story of redemption as Holy Spirit guided him. We were growing in our marriage and really exploring what marriage meant, what our roles were, and how we wanted to do things in our home.

This took a lot of communication on topics that we should have talked about before we were married, including family traditions and holidays. Our first family event happened to be the day we became engaged, on Easter. For some reason, I just assumed that he would know that when there was a holiday, we gathered with my family of over forty relatives. He happily came, and we enjoyed the wonderful afternoon at my aunt's home with delicious food and the fun Easter egg hunt for the children. After about four hours, I finally realized that he was ready to go. Eventually, more holidays came, including Thanksgiving, Christmas, and New Year's Day, with my expectation that we would spend them with my extended family. I assumed this without ever communicating it with him. When he asked why we weren't creating our own traditions, my response was, "This is how it's always been done and how it will be done." Ouch.

I did not even think to ask him what he wanted to do. I just told him what we would be doing. Communication fail. I was not hearing what he was trying to say and made him feel bad any time he would try and object.

Then came the discussion for the approaching Christmas Eve and what we would be doing. For me, Christmas Eve was a stay at home, get cookies ready, read *'Twas the Night Before Christmas*, and watch a movie type day. For him, Christmas Eve was a big deal with the family going to Church, having a delicious meal, and opening all of the gifts (Christmas morning was for Santa gifts). My response was," huh?". I did not mind planning and preparing the meal, and we had decided already that we were going to go to church, but opening all of the gifts on Christmas Eve I just couldn't do. Christmas Eve was for opening one present, always new pajamas, and that was it. In fact, to create more of a magical feel for Ashley, I never put presents from me under the tree until after she went to bed on Christmas Eve. If someone mailed gifts or something was received at school or wherever, they went under the tree. Then, on Christmas morning, it was pure magic and hearing the squeals and laughter was priceless.

The year before we were married, we attended a Christmas Eve service, he prepared a delicious dinner, and my mom came over to his apartment and joined us. I convinced him to not open presents that night, which did not take much convincing with alcohol. He enjoyed helping me set out the presents for Ashley, and things went as I anticipated.

This Christmas, it was different. We had our own home, our first child together, and no clear plan on what traditions for our family would look like. What do you do when you have one way of doing things, your spouse has another, and neither of you is wrong? The answer is pretty simple, yet something we had not done. You have to talk about your expectations and be willing to compromise. If I am being honest, I felt like I would be able to present my arguments for why I was right and then strong-arm him into changing his way to fit my way. That doesn't sound much like compromising to me.

We ended up talking through each holiday and what that would look like moving forward for our family. As the years have gone by, we have had to adjust some, but there is mutual respect and discussion about what the holiday will look like instead of each of us just assuming our way was the right and the only way. Our Thanksgiving tradition became us going to the large family gathering on Thanksgiving Day, and then the Friday or Saturday after Rich will cook a large Thanksgiving meal, and we invite family and friends over. Christmas was tough to compromise, and it took several years to find our fit. My compromise was opening the traditional pajama gift and one other gift that they select under the tree, which I would only put certain gifts out to make sure the selection was something that was appropriate to open early (clearly you can see that control thing I was talking about). We decided that for this season, we would no longer be going anywhere on Christmas Day because that was best for our family. We attend Christmas Eve church service and have a nice dinner. Rich continued on the tradition of reading *'Twas the Night Before Christmas* to our children, just as my dad had done each year as we were growing up. I promised to never buy him matching Christmas pjs or give him pjs for Christmas ever again.

The bottom line is that what has always been does not have to always be, especially within a family unit. Sometimes we do not even know why things are the way they are or why they matter so much to us unless we stop and examine the why. Reading a book on Christmas Eve was about remembering my dad, honoring him in a way, by keeping a tradition that he had participated in while alive.

I had not communicated that to Rich, and he did not know why it was important to me. I just assumed he would know. I think back to so many of our disagreements and how easily they could have been avoided if we had just taken the time to talk through things instead of making assumptions that the other would know. Once he understood, of course he did not mind continuing the tradition. In fact, he was honored to do so. What a difference a little talking can make!

We come from the same country, yet very different ways of doing things. We joke with one another that he speaks Colorado and I speak Virginia, he speaks man and I speak woman, and the same phrase can mean two very different things. A prime example of this was seen early into our relationship. We were heading on a road trip and got a flat tire. He pulled into a gas station in a little country town in North Carolina. It wasn't long before there were several men standing behind him, watching, and offering their help. Rich was polite and declined their help, assuring them that he was just changing the tire and we would be on our way shortly. Once we were back in the car, he was so angry that these men thought that he didn't know what he was doing, standing there watching him, and kept asking if we were all right. I was so confused. We both had been present for the same situation, yet we both took two very different things away from it. He felt completely disrespected, and I felt reassured that these kind men were there willing to help any way we needed. I explained that it was just a southern thing and they were not meaning any disrespect. In fact, it was the complete opposite. They did not want anything. They did not think he wasn't capable. They just wanted to help us if we needed it.

Another example is the ever-common southern phrase, "bless your heart." For those reading this in the south, you don't need any further explaining of this phrase with so many meanings. It really depends on the tone of the person who says it whether it is sincere, as in I really feel for you and I will pray for you, or an insult, as in you really have no clue. Southern (passive aggressive) charm.

It is not just phrases that can create misunderstandings and tension, but also male and female differences. Being that I was a single mother for nine years, I learned many things, and one was to not hesitate to ask for help, especially in a store. For one, I was usually in a hurry and did not have time to browse, so asking for help made shopping faster in stores like hardware stores. If I wasn't sure what to use, I would ask. I was not very handy when it came to fixing things. It only made sense to ask an employee for help or their advice on what to do. I had done this for many years, and it was second nature to me.

One day, we were in a large store buying materials for a project that Rich was going to work on, including drywall, 2 x 4s, and quite a few other things. He is a silent processor, thinking through each project, the materials he would need, the steps he would take, and the most efficient way to complete the project. He is a carpenter, extremely talented and filled with knowledge that was passed on to him from his father, who is also a carpenter. I interpreted his silent staring at the materials as "I'm not sure what to do." I couldn't have been more wrong, but I assumed my way was his way, and that his silence must mean the same thing as my silence. My instinct and learned behavior over the years kicked in, and in my helpful and loving way I proceeded to find an employee, bring them over to where my husband was standing, and tell him that I think my husband needed some help trying to figure out how to do this project. Oh southern, well-meaning woman, questioning her husband's skills in front of another man. As I was removing all confidence that he felt that I had in him, the employee opens his mouth and says the words that fell out like slow motion, 'Hey man, are you all right? What do you need help with?".

Bless my heart. Strike one.

He politely declined help and assured me he knew what he was doing. I did not even consider that my asking the employee to help him would translate into me thinking he did not know what he was doing. All was well, and as we were leaving, another store employee asked if we needed help loading the items into the truck. Rich said no thanks and that he had it. I stood there with the cart as he went to pull the truck up. Being the wonderful wife that I was, I decided to accept the help that the nice employee was offering. (As I am typing this, the whisper of, "crazy woman, didn't you learn anything from what just happened?" is in my head). He pulled up with the truck, and the employee, the same one that he had just declined assistance from, was standing there ready to load. Rich tells him thank you, but no thanks and explained that he had a certain way that he wanted to load it based on where things were going when he unloaded it. Note back to where I said that he is silently planning, knows exactly what he's doing, and has his own way of doing things. Not my way. His way. I hate to even type the next part. In a shining moment of glory, I objected, insisting that this employee does this all the time, he probably knows an efficient way to load, and two hands are better than one, as I stood there proud of myself for getting him help. You know, I was helping him by getting help, right?

Nope.
Uh huh.
Not even a little bit right.

Not only did I question his ability AGAIN, I suggested that this employee would know more than he did. I urged this unnecessary help and, in the process, completely emasculated my husband, who was looking at me in disbelief of what was happening. The employee quickly took Rich's side and said the he clearly knew what he was doing and that he had to get back inside. Oh no! I did it again! That was strikes two and three all rolled up into one package deal.

Blink.

Thankfully, one of my dear friends was at this same store and offered to give me a ride home. At least I realized that space was what this situation needed. Lots of space.

This friend was married to her high school sweetheart and had years of experience. I told her all about how helpful I had been and that I didn't understand why he was so upset. She told me that there were times to speak up and times to shut up. When he is in his element, doing something that he knows, then it's best to sit back and let him do his thing. She suggested that I did not need to interject my opinions and advice, especially when it was unsolicited advice, because it removes his role. She had been a friend for many years, had seen the ups and downs, and knew that I was used to figuring out ways to do things, even when I had no idea how. She told me that in order for this to not continue to be a problem that we needed to define our roles and that I needed to stop trying to control every little thing. I knew that she was right and appreciated her wisdom and guidance. Friends who will tell you the truth, even when it's hard to hear, are invaluable.

Once things cooled down, we were able to discuss things that we had both assumed we knew. We made some loose guidelines and talked about why we objected and then tweaked it until we agreed. We tackled issues like cooking and cleaning. Whoever cooks, the other cleans the kitchen. When it comes to cleaning, we are a team and both will work together to keep things neat and orderly, although I really feel like I won in this area because he offered to take the bathroom. For grocery shopping, I would do the majority of the shopping, though this has changed over the years to I will order them online and whoever is free can pick them up. When it comes to the children's doctor appointments, I would take them. Birthday and Christmas shopping would be my task, but we would both wrap. Yard work was his area, and I was glad to hand that over. Whatever works for your marriage, go with it. Just make sure that things are discussed to establish those roles, and if things need adjusting, then communicate and fix it. It's amazing what a little conversation can change.

I like to think of this phase of marriage as the infancy stage. We really knew nothing about how to do this life together, but we both knew we were determined to make it work. Four short months after Andrea was born, we were expecting our third child, learning to communicate, attending church every Sunday, participating in a weekly church group, and making strides towards better choices. Rich was taking classes at a university that was close by and working towards finishing his bachelor's, and I was taking classes online towards finishing mine. I think that we were so busy that it created a false sense of thinking we were better than we actually were. We hardly saw each other because we both worked full-time, he was off to school two to three nights a week, and we filled in every empty space on our calendar that we could because the more things, the better. The busier, the better. The more we said yes, the better. If we did not have something planned or on the calendar one night, then something must have gotten forgotten.

It's embarrassing to say that a girlfriend called and wanted to get together and it was well over a month away that I had an hour free. I had everything color-coded on the large calendar that hung in the kitchen. If it was not on the calendar, it did not happen. It became our communication to the point of not actually talking, but saying, "go check the calendar," in response to what we had going on the next day or over the weekend. Were we in a marriage, or running a business? It was hard to tell, and the problem, the big gaping problem that we could not see, is that we did not leave any room on the calendar and schedule for each other. We were like ships passing in the night, too tired to talk about the day or what the other was going through, and too busy to make it seem like we cared.

By every societal measure, we were successful. We had the home with a white picket fence. We had 2.5 children (literally because I was pregnant with number three). We had good-paying jobs. We were serving in church. We were great on the outside looking in. We were looking for things to fill our time, but made plenty of excuses when it came to making time for one another. At the end of the day, we would be so tired from all of the things we were choosing to fill our time with, we had nothing left to give each other. We stayed in this cycle for several months, adding more and more to our plates, thinking we were doing great, until those plates came crashing down around me. Something had to give, but how do you decide what to give up when you are enjoying everything you have going on? For me, it was the not so gentle reminder that my priorities were out of order and that I needed to go back to the basics of God, spouse, children, then everything else. That meant learning to say that dreaded word that had become so difficult for me...no.

CHAPTER 9
Identity Crisis

*E*ver since I was fifteen years old, I had at least one job. I did not like having to ask anyone for anything unless it was absolutely necessary. As an adult, I never had more than enough money and always lived paycheck to paycheck. I could find a deal for nearly everything, or I passed on the purchase and became a master of making one dollar stretch.

When Rich and I met, I was working as a contractor and making more money than I ever had up to that point. When I got word that the contracts for my type of position were going to be eliminated, I had the opportunity to move to another company with one of my former supervisors. During my pregnancy, they were wonderfully accommodating, and the job itself was enjoyable. However, every morning, dropping Andrea off at the babysitter, I would feel the urge to stay home with her. I knew there was no way that we could survive on one salary, and so I pushed the idea aside. As my pregnancy with Chloe progressed, I began to have signs that she was trying to come early. My midwife suggested I cut my working hours down to four-hour shifts. She ultimately took me completely out of work prior to delivery. I was able to collect short-term disability and, therefore, able to still contribute financially.

As much as I knew I had to go to work to maintain our lifestyle, I also knew that the prompting to stay home was growing louder and louder. When I mentioned it to Rich, he was surprisingly in agreement with the idea and felt stronger about it than I did. But how? In just two short years, we bought a house, got married, and had two children, making us a family of five. Babies are expensive, and we had two, and we had a preteen. How in the world could I stop working and cut our income in half? As the weeks passed and the end of my maternity leave was nearing, I knew we had to make a decision about what I was going to do. I went back to work, but only lasted two weeks before deciding it was time to give my two-week notice. Thankfully, Rich was able to work a lot of overtime by working on the weekends and long days. I learned the art of coupon clipping, shopping the sales at the grocery stores, and cutting out all of the things that we did not need. We realized it was going to be hard, but we also knew that God would make a way because we were certain that it was the right decision.

I knew how to do the working mom thing, but this stay-at-home mom idea was foreign to me. The new role was very awkward for me at first. I did not know what to do with my days so that I would feel like I had accomplished enough. No matter how many loads of laundry I did, how many tiny humans I took care of, how many meals I prepared, or how many hours I served, it never felt like enough. Rich was very thoughtful with letting me know how much he appreciated everything that I was doing around the house. He would say things like, "Would you like me to bring the laundry from the dryer in?". I would turn this seemingly innocent question into an obvious implication that I was not doing enough. His attempt to help lighten my load would end with a fight and me in tears, feeling like I was a failure. This was nothing he was doing. It was completely in my head.

I did not understand why I was feeling the way I was. Here I was, doing what I had always dreamed of, but never thought possible. God had made a way when we did not see one, but I was unhappy and feeling pretty worthless. There were many days that I would cry, not understanding why and really unable to explain it. I held it together in front of everyone because I did not want to appear weak or ungrateful for the opportunity that I had been given to stay with our children. One morning, I was crying out to God, asking why I felt like this. I didn't really feel better after praying, but I knew that I had to keep putting one foot in front of the other, going through the motions, and keep on smiling because that is what I do.

Never did I think God would answer my question in the middle of a grocery store. I was making the usual grocery trip to pick up a few things, and I felt the need to message Rich and ask him if it was okay for me to get groceries. His response was, "Of course, why would you need to ask to buy groceries?". I told him it was his money, and I didn't want to spend it without asking. I felt like time stood still, and I do not even remember what he said after that. I just knew that God answered my why.

Blink.

One moment I was Christy Hardin, productive and working member of society, and the next moment I was Christy Hardin, unemployed stay-at-home mom. For as long as I could remember, my identity and worth had been tied to a job title and paycheck.

In my mind, if I did not bring in an income, then *clearly* I was not productive and contributing to the needs of our family. When had my worth been so lost and minimized to that of where I worked? I was always striving for the next promotion and additional opportunities to help others at work, and I was always exceeding expectations, all to prove nothing. It never mattered what level I was. It wasn't enough, and I wanted more. I do not think there was a level that I could have reached to feel like I had made it. While part of this is just my nature to want to help others, another part was an attempt to make up for feelings of inadequacy and being less than others. Once I stripped away my title, my paycheck, my identity, there was an empty shell of a woman left not knowing who I was, or what to do now.

This realization happened in the middle of a grocery store, asking my husband if I could buy groceries. I managed to buy the groceries and get out to the car before losing it in the parking lot. I was still the same person. Or was I? Why was I letting money and some silly title define me and determine how I felt about myself? Here it was again, that ridiculous control issue of mine. For years, I had promised myself that I would never be in a position where I would not be able to support myself and my children. Me, me, me. It was all about my needs and the feeling of being in control of certain situations, especially when it came to my children. Somehow, in my mind, I was letting my children and family down because I was not doing anything to provide for them financially.

When I shared this realization with Rich, he looked at me like I had three heads. He then reminded me that there was no "his" money and "my" money. It was our money. He reminded me that first, I am the daughter of our King; there is no title that is more precious or important than that. I was reminded that my role of taking care of our children was something that we had both felt strongly about. I was able to be there for their firsts, to experience places with them, and be with them as they were growing up. I could be there for Ashley, getting her to and from school, after school, and in the summer. It took a near breaking point for me to see that my worth and value are not based on a salary or job title, as the world would have us believe, but it comes first from who I am in Christ and following the calling on my life.

As I embraced my new role, once I finally accepted it, I had a new outlook on my days. I was getting the opportunity to serve my family while serving the Lord. While there were many good days, the selfish side of me would come out at times and I would be jealous that my husband had a nice, quiet drive to work and had allotted himself at least thirty minutes each morning for Bible study and time with the Lord. It never failed that each morning that I attempted to get up to have that time there would be a sleepy-eyed toddler that would appear needing me. I resented the fact that he got to pick music over the same movie playing on repeat for the hundredth time. Of course I know that I am the adult, I am in control of the radio or movie selection in my vehicle, but there are some battles that are just not worth fighting. It sounds funny complaining about something that I am allowing to happen, but that's the truth. It wasn't Rich's fault or something that he was not doing, it was just the season of life for me that did not allow for much alone time while he was at work.

There were new expectations that would arise, and we found ourselves back in old disagreement patterns. He would work six days a week, often ten to twelve hours, come home and work on a project around the house or something outside. We had agreed, and I was very happy to do so at the time, that he would take care of the outside and yard upkeep. This meant that once a week, mainly in the summer, he would spend four hours mowing, edging, raking, cleaning, and whatever else needed to be done. On one hand, I was so thankful that he took such pride in our home and yard; on the other; I was typically inside trying to keep our very anxious children inside so that they would not delay the process. I became jealous of the fact that he got four hours to himself each week while I was "stuck." Being focused so much on what he had that I wanted, led to a slow building of resentment. Finally, I talked to him about it, and he explained that he wished nothing more than to be able to spend his time with our children and me, but he was doing what he thought would make me happy. All it took was a conversation about how I was feeling because he did not know, and I had expected him to read my mind.

There was a time that he would joke with me that we needed to drive two cars to church. Church was pretty much my only outlet for adult conversation outside of Rich and my mom. He was anxious to get home for quality family time, and I soaked up every moment of conversation that I could. Many times he would pick the children up from their classrooms and go wait in the van for me to eventually come out. My chatting on Sunday mornings would have to last until our group nights on Thursday, and I wanted all that I could get.

In the working world, I had plenty of interactions with co-workers, phone calls, and meetings. I never had the missing need for adult communication, until it was gone. In an effort to fill this void, there were many times I would turn to my phone, and it would be my companion as I would mindlessly play games or scroll through social media. For me, social media can be a wonderful way to connect with our family living across the country, friends I have not seen in a long time, and easily know what events are happening and where. It was also something that added to the feelings of loneliness. Most people, myself included, use social media to share pictures of events and travel, happy moments, and things you want others to see. I quickly forgot that these same people also have piles of laundry, dirty dishes, and some struggle with finding time for themselves, just as I had. I was filling my time becoming envious of the life others were portraying on a social media outlet. Then when I put the phone down, there were these little faces of my children who I had not been paying attention to. Ouch. The unmet need for social interaction and my loneliness had led to me missing out on the precious time I had with the precious lives that God had given to us to mold and shape. Was I molding them to look more like Christ, or more like my phone and the fake world that I was so wrapped up in?

Who was I? Honestly, I didn't know. I knew what I was missing, I knew whom I had given up, but who did I want to be for my children? Self-reflection can be so hard, especially when you do not know where or how to begin. I talked to Rich and knew that I was so busy caring for everyone else, loving it because that's just my personality, that I was spending no time caring for myself. Simple things like buying things for myself that I needed would be put on hold because someone else needed something more. Wanting to spend time with girlfriends made me feel guilty because I had convinced myself that I needed to be home. I was chatting with a friend about this one morning on the phone, and we both realized that a seemingly small thing, like underwear and bras, was not something that either of us had purchased in way too long. We were putting everyone else above ourselves, and that is fine for certain things, but at some point, enough is enough. It took us talking about something that isn't a regular conversation item to realize we were both in the same boat. We promised each other that we would budget in some undergarment money and follow through with the purchase. What's funny is that neither of us did that in the timeline we allotted, but eventually, it became so comical that we just had to. The conversations of, "Did you buy your bras yet?" would always end in laughter and serve as a reminder that yes, we matter as well.

I mattered, even though I was not sure who I was. I mattered to God, and I mattered to my family. While the season of life I was in looked different that it ever had before, my identity and worth was not less. The need for connection with my friends is what I thought was missing, but it was the connection with my Father God that was lacking. He had not gone anywhere. I was not making Him a priority. Instead of reading my Bible on the app on my phone in those moments, I was scrolling social media. Instead of saying a prayer when times were tough, I would numb my thoughts with images of someone else's highlights. No wonder I didn't know who I was. I was so focused on what I didn't have, what I was missing, and resenting others who did have those things, that I had not fully embraced my new role as a stay-at-home mom to our beautiful girls. I did not want this opportunity to be taken for granted. I had been called to stay home, to pour into their lives, and in this season, my time would look different, but God looked the same. My moments that I yearned for with Him would not be in hour chunks to be able to spend reading and working through different devotions, but God would meet me in the moments I had. Sleep and rest would be something I mourned, but He would provide supernatural strength that only comes from God. My mind and thoughts, actions and time, needed to be refocused and centered on the three things that mattered most; God, Rich, and my kids.

CHAPTER 10
Unanswered Prayers

My heart and mind were in a better place as I settled into the routine that became my new normal. I was active in a new women's ministry at our church, and I was connecting monthly with other moms, weekly with our church group and church services, and daily with God. I was feeling happier, and Rich and I had settled into a pretty normal, yet not too busy, routine that was working well.

We learned that we were expecting another baby, and we were so excited. We began talking about sleeping arrangements and how our once perfect-sized home was going to feel even more full. We were not sure where or how it would work. We just knew that we were excited and the minor details would work themselves out.

Sadly, I started to have cramps, and that all familiar feeling came rushing back. Our midwife saw me that day, and confirmed our fears that we had already lost this precious life. While our hearts were sad and we did not understand why, we were comforted that our precious baby was with Jesus, and while we would not be able to hold our baby this side of heaven, one day we would be reunited. It was extremely hard and we mourned this life, wondering if the baby was another girl or a boy. We had not told the children, so we did not have to explain things to them. No matter the length of time, no matter how short the pregnancy, this little baby changed our lives and is so loved.

Within a few months, we found out we were expecting again. After suffering two miscarriages, the last being so recent, we were very nervous. Once we made it past the first trimester, we found out that our fourth child would also be our fourth girl, Molly. This was my fifth pregnancy in three years, and it was taking a toll on my body. I was often tired and weak feeling, but what pregnant mom of two toddlers wouldn't be? I did not really think much about it and tried to rest when I could. One morning, as I stood up to wash dishes, I passed out in my kitchen. Thankfully it was very brief, as both babies were home with me. I called my midwife, and she wanted me to go right to the emergency room. After quite the ordeal with doctors trying to figure out what type of patient I would be, hematology or obstetrics, I ended up being admitted for observation and testing. The results showed that I was severely anemic and was experiencing very low blood pressure.

I knew that I needed rest. I had been praying for rest, but this was a forced rest that I had not anticipated. My superhero mom came to our rescue with the children, and Rich stayed with me to make sure that I was okay. After many tests, two blood transfusions and several iron infusions, I was able to go home. Our baby girl was doing great, and I had no signs of labor, which was a huge relief, as I was only four months pregnant. They asked that I include a visit to the high-risk pregnancy office to ensure things continued to go well. I was also to begin getting iron infusions on a weekly basis in hopes of increasing my iron levels to a healthy level prior to delivery.

As if that were not enough with this pregnancy, we found out that she was breech in my eighth month. I was determined to do everything in my power to make her turn, because controlling that was something that I thought I could do. Rich would come home from work and I would be upside down, lying off the side of the couch. I tried every method available, and the night before we were scheduled for an ultrasound to verify that she was still breech and then version to try and turn her around, we prayed over her. We asked God to turn her so that I would be able to have the natural delivery I wanted. Our prayers were answered, and that night we watched as she turned and was head down at thirty-eight weeks. I had read so many blogs and comments that said that turning was unlikely at thirty-eight weeks. So we were amazed as we watched my belly and could see her different limbs working hard to turn. I was so excited and thankful that our prayers had been answered. A few days later, she turned again and was back in the breech position. This time it was in my sleep, but when I woke up and felt her, I knew what had happened. I called my midwife, and she was not surprised, as everything about this pregnancy was a little more complicated than the others.

We scheduled yet another room at the hospital for our midwife and OB to come and try the version, but either way, she would be born that day. I was thirty-nine weeks and a few days, and they told me that the likelihood of the version being successful was low. We prayed together, we prayed over my belly, we had our friends and church praying, and I was confident that our prayers would be answered. I made the decision and was determined to suffer through whatever was necessary so that she would turn and things could go according to my plan. After enduring the most painful experience of my life with the version, including two natural and unmedicated deliveries, she became footling breech. At this point, there was no other option, but an emergency c-section. Things began happening fast, and the false sense of control that I felt I had was quickly diminishing. I was so thankful for the skilled doctors, nurses, and my midwife who walked me through everything as it was happening. I was taken back on the stretcher to the delivery room and, as you can imagine, was extremely nervous. Rich walked in shortly after, and I was comforted having him there, neither of us knowing what to expect. I was so angry that we had prayed and had done everything in our power to avoid this situation, yet here we were. I did not understand why, and I was frustrated, but at that point, there was nothing I could do about it. This was not in my plan, and I didn't know why God didn't hear my prayer.

After much effort on the doctor's part, they were finally able to get to Molly, and she was born shortly after we entered the room. There was no first baby cry; there weren't the oo's and aah's that we had been used to hearing from staff in our previous deliveries. Molly was not breathing initially. The umbilical cord was wrapped many times around her neck and had a knot, and she was in pretty bad shape. More nurses were rushing in, and Rich and I just looked at each other not knowing what was going on.

Blink.

I began to panic and kept asking what was going on and if she was okay. While he did not know what was going on, Rich kept reassuring me that she was okay and that we would see her soon. I did not realize that he was equally as worried about me, as my blood pressure had quickly dropped, and the loss of blood was becoming a concern. The nurses and doctors were tending to Molly, and another set of nurses and doctors were tending to me. Rich was beside me and was praying for everyone in that room.

Through those tense moments, however, we could still feel God's presence and His angels surrounding us. After what seemed like eternity, there were faint cries that we could hear, and then finally that loud, beautiful, perfect cry came, and the tears flooded both of us. Our precious girl was here, and it truly did not matter how she arrived because she was okay. This confirmed God was there and that He, combined with the wonderful doctors and nurses, saved our precious girl's life.

After a night of reflection and thankfulness, Rich began thinking about our prayers and my questioning why God did not answer our prayers. He realized and explained to me that God did answer our prayer. We were fervently praying that she would turn. She did turn, at thirty-eight weeks, which in itself is a rare thing. God then protected her by turning her again at almost thirty-nine weeks, which would ultimately save her life. Despite how much we tried to control the situation, He was always in control and protected her.

I hate to think what would have happened if we had tried to have her naturally. If I had forced the issue and been so determined to do things my way, I would have completely taken the opportunity for God to protect her. She has always been a firecracker, and we know God has big plans in store for her. Trusting God in the hard times or unknown takes strength and surrendering, both things I was still learning. Forcing our way, even when it is clear that it is not what God desires, can lead to harmful outcomes for us or for others.

This was a lesson for us about persistence and not giving up. We do not know the plans God has for us, but we can trust that He does have a plan. I have found times where I am tired or weary of praying for the same thing over and over, for the same person to find Christ, or for the same change in a situation. My grandmother and mom have joked with me that it was their prayers and not giving up on me that allowed me to make it through all of the situations I did. Even when it is hard, pressing in to God matters. Even when you do not think that God hears you, He is listening and knows what is best. An unanswered prayer does not mean no. It could mean not now or that He has something better planned for you. I am so thankful for my friend, who was persistent in asking us to church, praying for us to say yes. If she had stopped praying or had given up, we may have wound up on a completely different.

It is not always easy to accept unanswered prayers. I did not understand why God did not heal my dad from his battle with cancer. It has been helpful for me to think about it in a different way as I have matured in my faith and walk with Him. We were praying and believing for my dad to be healed, to be whole, and to be cancer-free. I have found peace in knowing that while I do not understand, I know that he is pain-free, whole, and with Jesus. Our time here on earth is but a blink of an eye, and I take comfort in knowing that we will be together for eternity. It is reassuring to imagine him being the one to welcome and hold our babies who are already in heaven.

I have prayed for many things that seemingly go unanswered. Much of the time, I am praying, giving God my desired outcome to the situation I am praying for, without leaving room for Him to work in the situation. The sooner I realize that God is the one in control and that He does not need my help to figure things out, the better I will be. I am a work in progress. That being said, it is important to pray specific prayers that are bold and clear, as we did with Molly. When we pray for specific things, such as my iron level to rise or my blood pressure to be stable, it gives us the ability to see God working in our lives. If we can take our requests to God just like we would a friend, thinking about why we are praying for what we are, to truly examine our hearts and desires, it will also help us understand ourselves.

In Mark 10:51-52 (NIV) is an example that Jesus gave about being specific with our requests by saying: "'What do you want me to do for you?' Jesus asked him. The blind man said, 'Rabbi, I want to see.' 'Go,' said Jesus, 'your faith has healed you.' Immediately he received his sight and followed Jesus along the road." The blind man didn't say, I want to be healthy; he said I want to see. When we go to our Father in prayer, He cares about each and every one of our needs and our praises. It is through a relationship with Him, that God knows our prayers, even when we do not know how to express them.

Sometimes when the answer is no or not right now, it is so hard to understand. While I wish I had the answers as to why some are cured from illnesses and some aren't, I don't. Why are some lives cut short while some live long, healthy lives? I don't know. Why do children and adults suffer unimaginable and excruciatingly painful situations? I don't know. What I do know is that we have a Father in heaven who loves us more than we can ever imagine, and He hurts when we hurt. While we do not know the answers to some difficult questions, we can rest in His promises, knowing that our eternity is with Him, in a place with no pain or suffering, where we will be fully restored and whole. He hears our prayers. He loves us, and He knows the outcome of our requests. That being said, sometimes our unanswered prayers eventually lead to some of our greatest blessings.

CHAPTER 11
Unexpected Meetings

When Rich and I got married, we had many conversations about how divorce would never be an option for us. We knew we did not have it all together, but we both had a desire to serve with our church marriage ministry. There was training that we completed to provide premarital counseling for couples, as well as mentoring couples who may be facing a rough patch. We worked with many couples, and I began mentoring several women. I'm not sure how it happened, but I seemed to know who needed someone to talk to. I found that many of the women were single mothers, and a desire to make a difference in this specific area began to grow within me.

As I neared the end of my degree, I was required to complete an internship. I searched several different organizations and decided that I wanted to complete my time at a local crisis pregnancy center. There was training that I had to complete, including call center training, and eventually working in the center with women who were pregnant. I was somewhat hesitant to go to a crisis pregnancy center because I had flashbacks of walking into the abortion clinic and the hatred that lined the sidewalk. There was no way that I would partake in anything like that, so I proceeded with caution. Everything I had built up in my mind about what it would be like was completely wrong. I walked into the center and met the most God-loving woman. She would eventually become one of my dearest friends to date. I watched her meet with women who were nervously excited to find out they were pregnant when she would administer a pregnancy test, to those who were devastated with the news of pregnancy and wanted to talk through the different options, and everything in between. There was never any judgment or feelings of condemnation, just genuine care and prayer.

I began meeting with the women and was able to share my story on several occasions. Although I did not feel that I was not able to share my story with anyone I knew, there was something about the transparency and vulnerability at the clinic that I could have with the women there. I was able to let them know that I had walked in their shoes and felt the weight of the decisions they would be making. The center offered classes for the women to learn how to be parents, and they could earn baby bucks to shop in the store that was filled with clothing, diapers, wipes, and things for the baby. There is a gap in our system for working, single parents. For many of them, if they work, then they make too much for help, but if they do not work, the help is not enough to survive. Help is limited and hard to find, and it can be humiliating to have to beg for help when all you want to do is raise the child that God blessed you with. Society is so quick to judge, yet so slow to respond to the cry for help.

After completing my internship, I wanted to do something more, but did not know what. We were barely making ends meet, and it was not easy to volunteer while having three small children and a teenager. I was speaking with one of my dear friends, and we both had a passion for single mothers. We were both single mothers and knew the struggle all too well. We may not be able to do much, but together we could do our best. Village 54 was the ministry that was born. The name of our ministry came from knowing that it took a village walking alongside each of us while we were single parents, and we used Isaiah 54 as our guiding scripture. We were able to provide groceries and mentoring for single mothers. We were able to help some of them with moving, locating furniture, and delivering it. Through community support, we provided Christmas for several single mothers and their children. We helped any way we could. We would receive messages about a need and then reach out to the community for help filling the need. It was amazing the outpouring from the community wanting to help others and the ability for those to ask for help without feeling shame or judgment.

I received a message from a friend saying she had met someone at church that she wanted to introduce me to. A little while later, another friend messaged me the same thing. After talking with both of them, I realized that they were both talking about the same person. They each had prayed and felt like I was supposed to meet her. We decided the four of us would meet later that week for lunch. I did not know it, but this meeting would change my life.

I walked in and was immediately drawn to this woman. Elyse was her name. I wanted to know her story and about her life. She explained that she went to a yard sale and there was a woman who kept asking her to go to church, and that she finally said she would go. She was skeptical of church and didn't really know if she believed in God. She had just arrived a few weeks prior after taking a bus from Las Vegas to Virginia to leave an abusive relationship. Once she arrived at her cousin's home in Virginia, she learned that she was pregnant. She grew up in a world that was completely different than mine, filled with everything you can imagine about Vegas. For much of her life, she could only depend on herself, and everyone always had an angle or wanted something.

Lunch ended up lasting over four hours as she shared about her life. It was clear that there was no coincidence in our meeting and that this was a God introduction. My friends did not know why they felt like I should meet this woman, but they both followed the prompting of God to introduce us. We exchanged phone numbers, and I already had thoughts in mind of how I could help her with her pregnancy. Later that week, I took her to the pregnancy center, where she began taking parenting classes and getting some of the much-needed supplies for her baby on the way. She continued to go to church, but was clear that she wasn't ready to make a decision about God until she knew more. Rich and I led a small group in our home and invited her to attend. She was hesitant, thinking she would not fit in or that she would feel judged and unwelcomed, as she had so many times in the past. One Sunday after church, Rich and I decided to have a little cookout and invited some of our friends from church, including Elyse. As we were sitting around talking, Elyse was getting to know another friend of ours who just radiates joy and the love of Jesus. The genuineness and welcoming behavior were confusing for our new friend, and she actually asked why this person was being so nice to her when she didn't even know her. Elyse could not understand someone just wanting to build a friendship with her without wanting or expecting anything in return. However, I think she began to see that maybe we were more alike than we were different.

After the cookout, Elyse was more comfortable with the idea of trying our small group. When she walked into her first small group meeting, she quickly saw that we were real, transparent, and open with one another. We shared our burdens and prayer requests, as well as celebrated victories throughout the week. It was a place free of judgment, but with relationships who would be honest with one another. She was eager to learn about the Bible and wasn't afraid to ask questions when something would come up that she did not understand or agree with.

The following Sunday, Elyse felt an overwhelming presence of God and became a Christian, asking for prayer from one of the leaders. It doesn't take much to be nice to people, and it broke my heart to know that so many had judged her based on outward appearance or from mistakes of her past. It's so easy to focus on what someone has done wrong. Imagine if we took the time to look past that, find out what we have in common, and celebrated what they have overcome.

At the time we met, she was not working and did not know what type of job would provide enough support for her to be able to move from her cousin's home. We created her resume, and the job hunt began. I called the cofounder of Village 54 and explained that I felt we needed to help Elyse, but I just did not know how. We prayed, and the three of us met to talk. We talked about job options and steps to create a new life for Elyse. She had the unique opportunity to live in a new area and have a fresh start. As her pregnancy progressed, she became concerned that she would have a difficult time finding a job, as she was already showing. We prayed and believed that she would find the perfect job. She was also concerned about finding a job that she could take the bus to because she did not have a car.

Through word of mouth at church, she learned of a company that was not too far from where we lived. She would be able to sit down while working and she would not have to do shift work. She called and was able to schedule an interview. I drove her to the interview, and as we pulled up, she grabbed my hand and asked me to pray with her. The peace and confidence she exited the car with could be seen, and I knew that she would soon be employed. While she was inside, I drove around and realized that the building was less than two blocks from Rich's job. I began to pray, in anticipation that she would be hired that day, for her hours to align with Rich's so that he could bring her to work and pick her up after work. The same day she interviewed, they offered her a position with similar hours to the hours Rich worked. He turned his once morning alone time with Jesus into a time to minister to Elyse on their daily drive to and from work

One night that summer, Elyse called me saying that some things had come up and that she didn't have anywhere to go for the night. I went and picked her up and brought her to our house. Coincidentally, Ashley had already left that summer for a six-week mission trip in Haiti. Rich and I talked it over and offered for her to stay in Ashley's room while she was gone. Like I said, God's timing is always perfect, even if we do not see it at the time.

I took her to open a checking account, and she was so proud of this accomplishment. For some, this is no big deal. For Elyse, this was a turning point and another chapter in her redemption story.

My mom, who has always had a way of loving my friends in such a special way, wanted to take Elyse to the DMV, and she beamed with pride to call and tell me that Elyse had passed the driving test and was now a licensed driver. She took a picture of her in front of the DMV, and Elyse was so overcome with emotions for several reasons. First, she had to overcome some obstacles that once seemed impossible for her to get her driver's license and second, she felt the motherly love and pride from my mom that she had not experienced before.

Life was turning around for her, but the lingering problem remained about what she was going to do when her baby girl arrived and what would she do when Ashley returned home. We searched and searched for a home or apartment for her to rent that would overlook some rental history concerns and less than perfect credit. Each time we would look at an apartment or house, it was either way out of her budget or putting her in the middle of a lifestyle that she had escaped. We prayed with Village 54, and I talked with Rich, brainstorming and talking about every possible scenario, and we just couldn't find a solution. It wasn't until I prayed specific, bold prayers for God to help us find a solution that something miraculous, something that only could come from Him, happened.

The next morning, I woke up and knew that we needed to find her an apartment that would be paid for her for six months, somewhere she could bring her baby girl home to that was safe and their own. The only problem was I did not have a job, and there was certainly no way that Rich and I could afford to do that.

Do you ever have those conversations with God where you are like, "okay, I hear you, but that is ridiculous, and there's just no way"? Arguing with God and putting Him inside the little box of realistic possibilities that I had planned did not work so well for me. I really feel God must laugh at my sarcasm and questioning whether I heard from Him or if I was forcing an issue. The difference is pretty easy to determine because when it is from God, He finds a way to make it happen, no matter how hard we resist. Oh how easily we forget that nothing is impossible with God. I knew it would take help, but who? Who would be willing to give me money for this crazy idea? I decided to pray and just write down names that came to mind. I told Rich what I felt like I was supposed to do and how crazy I felt doing it. Some of the people on the list did not even know Elyse, but it was clear whose names were supposed to be on that list. I composed an email about our unlikely encounter, which was obviously God-inspired, and a little about her. I shared my heart for wanting to help her and really felt like she needed the chance for a fresh start. God was moving in her life, and sharing her story was easy.

She had more disappointment and heartbreak in her life than anyone should, and I did not want to add to that if this plan did not work out. I decided to keep everything under wraps and made sure everyone that I emailed knew that she did not know what was going on. I have been known to pull off a few surprises, but this was going to take some real work. She continued searching for apartments and homes, and we rode around for countless hours in hopes of finding something. In the meantime, I began a separate apartment search that Elyse did not know about. We settled on a complex that was less than a mile from where we lived, and they were willing to let Rich sign a six-month lease, having Elyse as the resident. Now we just needed to keep praying and trust that God would move in the hearts of those receiving the email. I asked them to consider donating fifty dollars each month for six months to pay for an apartment. Asking people for money is not an easy thing to do, much less for something that would be an ongoing commitment for half of the year from people I did not know well. However, asking for help from people who God placed on your heart to help someone in need is easy. It's amazing what a group of people can accomplish together instead of trying to do it alone.

One by one, the emails started coming in with an overwhelming amount of support and promises of donations. We received a large donation that would end up being exactly what we needed for the down payment to secure the apartment. I was just blown away with the generosity of others and how all of us working together was actually going to make it happen. It was so important that we gave God the glory and continued to praise Him for making a way when we did not see one. This was God's plan, and we were being His hands and feet, putting into place what He had orchestrated. Rich and I went to sign the lease and pick up the keys. The woman at the leasing office was brought to tears when we shared with her the beautiful blessing and opportunity that was being given to Elyse and her future daughter. That day, we had the opportunity to go and pray in her empty apartment.

While the apartment itself was wonderful, God had more planned. We put the need out on the Village 54 social media page and asked for donations to furnish an apartment. We were looking for furniture, kitchen necessities, a bedroom set, dressers, crib and nursery furnishings, and home décor. You name it, we needed it. We spent many nights preparing her apartment, including printing out pictures of her loved ones. She was still living with Rich and I, and I kept making up places to go at night so that she would not suspect anything. We invited everyone who had a role in supporting her to the apartment for the big reveal, from the ladies from the pregnancy center, to those who had been praying alongside us, to those who were donating financially monthly, and those who had provided furnishings for the apartment.

It was my job to distract her and keep her occupied while everyone arrived. We decided to go complete her baby registry, but the first store we went to, the computers were down. We drove to another location and wandered around picking things out for her registry. When we were finished, I needed to find a way to pass more time. I knew that she was starving and asked her if she wanted to go get some dinner. Just as we pulled into the parking lot of her favorite restaurant, I got the message that everyone was there and waiting for us. I had to come up with a story as to why we needed to leave. What a cruel thing to do to a pregnant woman! She was trying to be nice, but I know she was hungry and just wanted to eat. I told her that my friend needed us to come over to help with something right then.

We pulled up to what would be her new home, and she wanted to stay in the car. I asked her to come with me so I could introduce her to my friend. We walked up the stairs to the apartment, and I knocked on the door. Rich opened the door and said, "Welcome home, Elyse!"

Blink.

She was so confused as to why Rich was there when we walked in to what she thought was my friend's apartment. Still confused, she looked around, seeing some familiar and also unfamiliar faces, not really understanding what was going on. Once I was able to explain to her that this was her home, her own place that God and those around her were providing for six months rent-free, and where she would bring her baby, she was absolutely overcome with emotions. To see the genuine disbelief and thankfulness on her face that people would help her, without expecting anything in return, giving her a chance for success, and wanted nothing but the best for her was a moment that I will never forget. Imagine if more people listened to God when there was a need, came together, and found a solution. There is nothing impossible for God, and when we come together as the church, amazing things can happen. If those ladies had not listened to God to make the introduction, the relationships would not have been formed. Something so seemingly small transformed someone's life.

Elyse no longer lives in our area, but we stay in touch. She is like family to me, and I am so thankful for our time together. She taught me about resilience, and while we lived totally different lives, we are all God's children. I have told her many times how her friendship changed me for the better. The conversations we had, sitting in our pajamas on my couch, about God, hard questions, and the obstacles we have both overcome were some of the most real conversations I have ever had. She gave me a chance, just like I gave her a chance, neither letting our pasts define who we are today. For years, she had been told, directly or indirectly, that she had made too many mistakes, done too many bad things, and would never be able to change. I am pretty certain that she would be one of the first to tell you that her own forgiveness was one of the hardest things she would attempt to overcome in her lifetime. Forget the bad choices, the substances, the situations she had faced, it was the inability to forgive herself that haunted her at night. She believed the voices in her head and those who had told her directly that she was just too bad and forgiveness was just too far away.

We talked about the freedom that only Christ can give and that once she asked for forgiveness, she was forgiven. This was a concept that was extremely hard for her to understand because of everything she had ever been told or learned. Rich was able to share one of his favorite verses with her about God rescuing him and while their stories were obviously different, they ultimately were much the same. Psalm 40:1-3 says "I waited patiently for the Lord; he turned to me and heard my cry. He lifted me out of the slimy pit, out of the mud and mire; he set my feet on a rock and gave me a firm place to stand. He put a new song in my mouth, a hymn of praise to our God. Many will see and fear the Lord and put their trust in him." Through these conversations, we all were reminded of God's love and the power of His forgiveness. Those times we felt completely alone, God was with us. Those decisions we made to numb our pain, God was with us and hurting just as much, if not more than we were. I learned so much about God's healing power through her willingness to be vulnerable, exposing the darkest parts of her sins to us, while confessing them to God, and the healing that came from it. She explained that for all those years of bad choices, she felt alone and shame thinking about those she had wronged. Looking back, she could see where tough love was given by those closest to her, as well as uncalled for condemnation and the subject of much gossip.

She had given up on herself, and it was when she reached rock bottom that she found Jesus and the faces of those who were there to help her get back on her feet. She taught me so much about the importance of friendship and not ignoring a need or person that is in my life just because it is hard or takes my time. She knew that I had certain boundaries that were nonnegotiable, but she would be met with love and grace instead of hatred and judgment. Her friendship and amazement that I did not give up on her serves as a reminder about taking the risk to help someone in a situation that may be hard. Elyse knows that she is forever a part of my family and that I will always be there for her. She also knows that I am a person she can turn to for guidance in various situations or if help is needed and that I will always direct her back to God. I know that she will always be in my corner and that not many people can make me laugh like she can. God arranged our meeting. He directed the steps. He gave her the freedom and forgiveness that she thought was unattainable. He restored and renewed broken relationships that seemed unimaginable. The same God that did not give up on her, did not give up on me. While we are worlds apart, we are sisters in Christ and nothing can change that. What started as a simple conversation with someone different than me, led to a life-changing friendship, her finding God, and a reminder for me to take the chance on others that God places in my life.

CHAPTER 12

Be Still

The next phase of my life I like to refer to as the blur years. Rich and I had two more children, making our family complete rather quickly. We currently have five girls and one boy. You can probably now understand how having five young children at home could cause life to become a blur. Fortunately for me, I have learned to function on very little sleep. Rest is not something that I feel comfortable with for some reason. I actually don't sleep well at all. I multitask constantly, and I rarely am able to turn my brain off. I know that everything I have to do will still be there no matter what, but I get overwhelmed with trying to handle it all, and that is when depression can creep in. There isn't some magic pill that makes it all go away, especially with a large family. I just have had to learn how to create balance and reprioritize my life. This was challenging in the beginning. I was forcing myself to get up out of bed, to keep going when I didn't want to, and crying out to God to please just give me strength to get through the day.

One morning, as I was staring at a pile of laundry, completely overwhelmed with the task, I heard His whisper, "just be still." Of course, I thought, I am being still. I was still standing there, still looking at that pile of laundry, and it was still there. I like to think God enjoys my sense of humor and just shakes His head at me. Clearly, I knew He didn't mean for me to just stand there still, looking at the laundry. So, I decided to sit on it, literally. Sitting on the laundry, I pulled up the Bible app on my phone, and Psalm 46 is where I turned.

"God is our refuge and strength, an ever-present help in trouble. Therefore, we will not fear, though the earth give way and the mountains fall into the heart of the sea, though its waters roar and foam and the mountains quake with their surging. There is a river whose streams make glad the city of God, the holy place where the most High dwells. God is within her, she will not fall; God will help her at break of day. Nations are in uproar, kingdoms fall; he lifts his voice, the earth melts. The Lord Almighty is with us; the God of Jacob is our fortress. Come and see what the Lord has done, the desolations he has brought on the earth. He makes wars cease to the ends of the earth. He breaks the bow and shatters the spear; he burns the shields with fire. He says, "Be still, and know that I am God; I will be exalted among the nations, I will be exalted in the earth." The Lord Almighty is with us; the God of Jacob is our fortress."

Be Still. It was one of those days where the enemy was having a good time with my thoughts. It was when I was still that I heard God telling me to be still.

Clearly, I am a bit hard-headed and have studied this verse enough that it should be on my mind. I have spoken these words to others, prayed it for many, and yet, I had forgotten it for myself. I decided that I needed a visual reminder that I could easily look at in those moments that overwhelm me. Ashley and I went together and got tattoos that read "be still," because we both can forget that in those hard moments. He is always there, ready to re-balance us and re-center our thoughts. Turning to Him is easy; for me, it's remembering to do so that seems to be where I get off track.

That pesky control issue and feeling like I have to figure things out on my own often takes over. Those negative thoughts about our outward appearance, comparison to others, feelings of being overwhelmed with daily to do lists, or whatever the enemy uses to take over our minds have got to go. Victory comes when we are able to stop those thoughts that bombard us and fix our minds and thoughts to those that are pleasing to God and filled with His truths.

Stop those thoughts. If only it were that easy. There have been so many times that I wish I could have turned off the thoughts of being overwhelmed, frustrated, confused, lost, lonely, and plenty of other feelings depending on the situation. I was living in a house full of people, people who were my children and husband that I love dearly, yet felt more alone than I ever had before in my life. Motherhood can be so lonely and for me there were more lonely times than not for a while. I found myself in the cycle of longing for relationships that I once had, to wanting to go somewhere, anywhere, to get out of the house, to not wanting to leave because it was too hard to round everyone up and I could pretty much guarantee a meltdown of enormous magnitude from one of the kids. The highlights of my day would be when the doorbell rang and the almost daily Amazon box was delivered. My delivery drivers see me a lot, and they even get a Christmas card and present because they are there so often to bring packages. When online grocery shopping became a thing, it was life-changing, and the need to go out of the house was less and less. There would be times when I did not leave my home for days because I did not really have a reason to. Yoga pants and Rich's t-shirts were my work attire, and I was stuck in the monotony of feeding someone, changing someone's diapers, the never-ending laundry cycling, cooking, and cleaning.

Having so many children certainly provides many opportunities for lessons from God. As I was leaving the post office one day, there was the all too familiar car seat battle with Molly. She did not want to be in her car seat, and I did not want to be at the post office any longer, as we had already mailed our package. She never particularly enjoyed being in the car, and I had pretty much come to expect a struggle. As I was wrestling her into her car seat in the parking lot, I turned around to a police officer. He had received a call about a possible abduction because there was a struggle happening. My first thought was, "Seriously? The person who called clearly does not have children." I explained what was happening and that my daughter was putting up quite the fight to be buckled into her seat. I asked him to please help me because I just did not have the strength. He felt sorry for me and tried to help me get her in, commenting how strong she was for such a little girl. I can only imagine what this must have looked like to those passing by. While the story is quite comical now, I think back about how I could have changed that situation. I was in such a rush, to go nowhere really, that my frustration was amplified. I did not stop and pray first before talking to her about her seat. I did not ask God for help. I just tried to force the situation.

Things were so overwhelming, and I felt like I was barely surviving each day. If you had asked me at the time, I would have told you everything was great, because I did not want anyone to think that I was not succeeding. I was not being honest with myself, much less anyone else. One day, Rich came home from work, and I had had one of those days. You know the kind I am talking about where everything that could possibly go wrong did, times two? He walked in, and I was ready to quit, throw in the towel on this mom thing. I was done. Clearly, that was not an option. But how in the world could I get through this when I felt like I could not do it another day?

My saving grace that day, and most days during the blur years, was Rich taking over bedtime. I knew that if I could make it to after dinner, then I could make it through the day. Rich came in like my knight in shining armor to give the kids baths, get them ready for bed, and then get them to sleep. It became my glorious time to do whatever I wanted or needed that day. Often, it was sitting in silence, reading my Bible or Bible study, and having that time with God.

I recently had a conversation with a friend about hot food. I am not used to it, and it is often alarming when I sit down to eat and the food is still at least warm. Having so many children, it works best for me to fix the plates and then put them on the table. This helps with rationing the portions and making sure one child does not get more than the other because, heaven forbid, that would be tragic. By the time they get their plates, Rich gets his, I get up four hundred and thirty seven times to get one's drink, one's fork that dropped, clean up the milk that was spilled, fix a new plate for the one that somehow managed to drop theirs on the floor, and all the other reasons, usually people are finished eating and mine is nice and room temperature. This is not a complaint because I know that one day my dining room table will be too quiet, and it will be Rich and I sitting there reminiscing about the good ol' days.

There are different seasons, and as one comes in, it takes adjusting and rearranging of expectations and responsibilities in order to get through them successfully. While the nighttime routine has changed, Rich still makes sure everyone is in bed after they shower and run through their nightly rituals. Being that he wakes up extremely early for work, I have found that nighttime is my time. I am able to do my college coursework uninterrupted, watch what I want on television, and read and study my Bible. I do have several friends who are night owls, and we can chat about what is going on in one another's lives. But those calls are few and far between. There's a lot of quiet. There's a lot of loneliness. The blur years were when I first knew I needed more interactions with women, particularly likeminded women who were in similar stages of life, women who would understand what I was going through, and, most importantly, women who could grow together in Christ. With all of the talk about finding your tribe, your circle of women who are there for you when you need to laugh or cry, need advice or need to be reminded of the hard things, finding this seemed nearly impossible. How and where would I start, especially in this season of life where I was in the thick of things with our kids? Where in the world would I find this? I did not know, but I knew that I needed to figure something out. As I prayed to God for answers and for help, He was already working and laying the foundation for things to come.

CHAPTER 13
The Great Awakening

I watch my kids on the playground, able to go up to another child, and with a simple, "Do you want to play with me?" off they go. A new friend is made and the ease of the relationship just flows naturally. As we get older and join things like sports teams, the camaraderie and team mentality help foster those budding relationships, and by the end of the season, there are usually great bonds made. Then comes middle school and high school, where the groups are formed and cliques emerge. We then learn where we fit in and where we are not welcome, and it is often heartbreaking to not be invited in to the group we think that we want to be in. This fragile time, even for the most popular crowd, can be nerve-racking, and one wrong social move can be damaging. I would like to think that we can create foundations that are solid so that our children, when approaching this formative time in their lives, have the confidence to be themselves, making friends based on character and similar interest, no matter what groups they are in. We have the unique opportunity to teach our children that while everyone may not be their cup of tea, that doesn't mean that they are less than or that it is okay to be rude or mean to one another. Finding our people becomes harder and harder as the years go by, but that does not mean that they aren't out there.

As a stay-at-home mom, I found that there were certain groups that I was welcomed into, but that also came with requirements that were over the top demanding and had an almost high school clique mentality. The general rules of parenting and what they deemed acceptable mothering ruled the flow of the groups and conversations. Dare I admit that I gave my child a pre-packed lunch or cereal for dinner (again), or do I just keep quiet? It was easy to revert back to those middle and high school days, trying to remember which group felt a certain way about one of the hot topics of parenting and fit in.

In my time of being lonely and not really sure where I fit in, I knew that this was not what I was after. Who had I become and why was I feeling like this? Where were my people? How could I find them? I couldn't be the only one feeling like that, but the age-old question of what do I do with this revelation and how can I move forward with it was present. I began with self-reflection and why I was feeling this way. It was because I was not being myself, and when I was, there were few that I could do that with.

Thankfully, my realization of this became evident, and the less I tried to force things with the wrong people, the easier it became to be myself with the right people. It is not always easy, and sometimes it takes putting yourself out there and asking a new person to have coffee or out to lunch. If you don't click, don't force the issue, and rest assured that it is okay. Be yourself and be real. It is pretty easy to determine if this was a fun use of an hour of your time or the beginning of a new friendship. I am certainly not an introvert, but it can still be uncomfortable to go up to someone you don't know well and invite them for coffee. Channel your inner 4-year-old at the playground and invite them to play, and I bet more times than not, they are eager to find a new person as well.

I was talking with two of my dear friends, and we felt this to be a common trend. Women were feeling the need for connection, genuine connection, with one another without knowing how to do that. The three of us had vastly different personalities, but together we meshed beautifully and knew that our vision was something to act on. As we prayed, the desire and talks of what we should do became something that God formed through the three of us. We had a planning meeting to brainstorm and collaborate our ideas that God had planted in each of us. The main theme that God made clear to us was women are yearning for ways to develop relationships with other women to help them grow in their walk with the Lord; they are yearning for support in that process, as well as the everyday highs, lows and in-betweens of life; they are yearning for a safe place for transparency and being vulnerable while building strong connections with one another. We knew this, but we didn't know how in the world to do that. What exactly were we being called to do? It all sounded a bit overwhelming at first. However, for me, any time that the Lord has given me an idea that could only come from Him, the how part comes naturally. This was no different.

Blink.

Through more prayer and discussion among the three of us, support from our husbands, and trusting God's direction, our ministry was formed. We brainstormed names for some time and left our first meeting to pray about the future of what we were forming. Awake. Awakening. Awaken. A quick internet search shows the meaning of awaken includes: to enliven, call forth, stir up, ignite, to stop sleeping, to become aware. It encompassed what we were going after in our ministry. We wanted to light a fire in the hearts of women we would reach and provide support, understanding, and encouragement in their quest for restored faith and a bold courage to allow God to guide their steps in various directions. Our vision, while following His direction, birthed the idea of having women's retreats. We had the idea of women getting away, retreating from life, to allow God to restore and recharge them, while also being challenged to self-reflect and become more aware of the areas where God shows them that growth is needed. This would take creating a place that was safe and free from judgment of one another, allowing for walls to come down and for opportunities for vulnerability. We talked about an afternoon gathering, but decided that there was no way to form actual bonds that weren't superficial in that short time. We wanted more, women wanted more, and God wanted more for this ministry.

We narrowed down our thoughts and ideas to a weekend retreat at a less than two-hour drive from where we lived to the Outer Banks in North Carolina, where we would rent a home, provide meals, and each share messages that we believed God would impart upon us. Of course there were doubts that crept in because when the enemy is worried about the Lord's work, he goes into action. We battled through thoughts of what if no one signs up to come, who would want to pay to hear us talk, and what if we let them down. Each time one of us was feeling a certain way, we voiced it to the others, and we would talk through it and pray. We knew deep down that this was a God thing and trusted that He would handle the details. When we announced the first retreat, we had space for twenty ladies, and we came up with a modest fee that would cover the rental home, food, materials, and goodies to give away. We met at my house, prayed about the cost, and decided to share our ideas on social media to spread the word and announce Awaken Ministries. Within 48 hours, the spaces were filled. Filled! We were so excited to see how God was working, and there was a clear need that we had tapped into, believing that we could create an awakening in women for God.

The yearning for more, for time to get away and to focus on self, and to find people that did not have expectations of you in order to accept you was real, and we actually had a waitlist for participants. The idea of going back to our childhood, those days of pajama parties with your girlfriends, just sitting around talking about life, playing games and laughing, was exciting to look forward to now as adults.

The enemy came in fast and hard. One of the founders was nearing the end of her pregnancy with her beautiful baby girl and came down with a horrible stomach flu that landed her in the hospital the evening before the retreat. As much as she wanted to be there, her health and that of her baby was most important. We knew that she would be praying for us and us for her as we arrived at the beautiful beach home.

Once everyone arrived, we announced that she would not be able to attend, and that she needed our prayers. There were women from all over Virginia, many who had never met one another, and some from as far away as Arizona who came to our first retreat. It was a true blending of women of all ages, races, backgrounds, and family settings. Each came with her own worries, excitement, and hesitations. For some of the ladies, their only connection was with the cofounder who was unable to come, and they were left not knowing a soul. In most situations, this could be a pretty big deal and make things extremely uncomfortable, but by the time we got through the first icebreaker to get to know one another, there was a house filled with laughter, introductions, and the realization that we were accepted and safe. The heavenly aroma of homemade lasagna that one of the ladies blessed us with was also helpful in easing everyone's mood that night.

The weekend ended and, without giving away anyone's story, healing occurred, years of bondage was released, and freedom was found. Our desire to know our Lord on a more personal level grew in leaps and bounds. We worshiped and sang our hearts out without fear of judgment or worry about what others were thinking. We had an overwhelming recharging of our minds and souls. We were awakened and could not wait to continue the friendships that began and to start planning the next retreat.

After the retreat, we sent out an anonymous survey to see where we could improve and what areas were enjoyed. The comments from the women brought me to tears as we received confirmation over and over again that we were following God's plan for this. One of the comments was, "I was anticipating creating new relationships with Godly, like-minded women and enjoying some time away from the kids to truly relax. Boy, was I wrong. I experienced SO MUCH MORE! Yes, my Sister circle grew and I feel rejuvenated, but God was moving in that house! So many testimonies. So many broken vessels coming together to share our brokenness. So many chains broken. So many tears, but just as much laughter! So much JOY! I will never forget the freedom I found this past weekend. Never will I pick back up the chains. Never will I hide behind the labels given to me by others. I will forever stand in confidence, knowing who I belong to and who I am because of I AM! I am on fire for God! My passion is reignited! I am preparing to live out my purpose like never before! God has Awakened the Spirit in me and I am not looking back!" Another survey said, "It was a blessing to open up with other women about things I struggle with and want to work on. I was able to share without feeling judged and ashamed. I was encouraged and now have an accountability partner to help me through difficult times. I was so blessed by hearing everyone's stories. We all have struggles. We all have pain that is very real to us. It shows up in our lives in different ways - but we have that in common. We are not alone! And that is a huge encouragement!"

We did not ask permission from anyone other than God to do this. We had no special training to lead women's retreats. It was God who gave us a united vision and acted on what we felt led to do, and the impact and reach was and continues to be far and wide. There have been several more retreats, more women have attended, and everyone is welcome. We have started having monthly gatherings to be intentional about getting together, and the ladies are encouraged to bring friends. The point is that it did not take special training or having financial backing from an organization to make a difference. All it took was listening to God.

Awaken has evolved over time, and through moves, new babies, life changes, and various other reasons it may look a little different, but the foundation is solid, and the vision to reach women as Christ called us to remains. I believe that this is a real need and want of women in our communities, no matter where you live, and if you wait for someone else to step up and create the ministry, it may never happen. Share your dreams and big, bold, God-given ideas with your friends. He may be speaking the same thing to all of you, waiting for you to join together and put your ideas into action. When this began, my once small circle of friends, I'm talking about the real friends who ask how you are and are genuinely interested in how you are, grew exponentially. I found my people!

One of the things that stands out to me at our Awaken retreats is how the groups of ladies always mesh together despite the vast differences among us. I once heard that if all of your friends look the same and fit the same category, age, race, and stage of life, then the first thing you should do is find ways to expand your friend list. It would be pretty obvious to say that most people stick with what is familiar. In doing so, we miss amazing relationships that are right there in front of us. How often do we find reasons not to be friends with someone or just assume they would not understand our life and make no effort to even talk to them, much less attempt a friendship? We have an internal dialogue and build a case against the person, focusing on the flaws we believe are there instead of having external dialogue with the person to find out about them. When all of the ladies are interacting, there is none of this. The women are sharing their lives and finding ways that they can relate to one another, and the commonalities become more and more apparent. The stories and situations become opportunities for others to chime in with "me too." It is as if you can see the weight of the chains cut and burdens being lifted as the almost overwhelming presence of the Holy Spirit fills the home. We are all daughters of the King. That should be what defines and unites us.

I would like to think that this is only the beginning of what God has in store for Awaken. I do not think there will ever be a time where women do not need each other and crave a way to connect on a deeper level, to find a mentor or someone who has walked through something that is similar to what you are going through, to be there with a shoulder to cry on while we go through hard times, to show up with soup and Lysol when the flu hits your family (you know who you are my dear friend), to hold you accountable and meet you at the track to train for your first 5K, to celebrate tremendous accomplishments such as graduations and new jobs, and to be ready to pray for everything in between. We all need a group to share real life with, without fear of judgment, where the truth can be told, even when it is hard, knowing it comes from a place of love and after prayer. If you do not have a group like that, Awaken Ministries has a place for you.

CHAPTER 14

Puzzle Pieces

Sitting in that same parking lot of the doctors' office after receiving the diagnosis of autism for Andrea, it was God I sought for guidance. Would we allow a diagnosis to change the direction of her life or would we work together to seek God with how to best help our girl? I knew that with Rich by my side, we would do everything possible to help all of our children, no doubt about it.

When I did not have the words or couldn't envision the next step, I reached out to one of the co-founders of Awaken, trusting her words and prayers to comfort my mind. God used our church group to connect us, and we built upon that relationship. We listened to Him to create Awaken, and these would become the sisters who keep my family lifted in prayer, as I do for them. His master plan is filled with intentional meetings and circumstances. It's almost as if our lives are made up of thousands of puzzle pieces, and they don't fit together until the time is right. Each piece has a purpose, design, and place in our lives. When you try and force a piece with the wrong match, it just doesn't work, and that is okay because there is another place for it. The more we try and force things, the more frustrated we become. When you are putting a puzzle together, it's pretty easy to tell when a piece fits and when it doesn't. Learning to trust my puzzle and allowing him to move the pieces is one of the greatest challenges I have had in my life. Someone else's pieces do not fit in my puzzle. I have my own to work with. We are each uniquely created and made, for His purpose, on purpose.

I did not intentionally use a puzzle as a metaphor because of the autism link, but it's just another example of God's direction and guiding of this book. Andrea is high functioning, and once I tell someone that she has ASD, I frequently hear that they would have never known. We are focusing our attention on helping her through social situations and circumstances that she may not understand. Her need to understand every detail before something happens is not something that she can help, but we can help her learn to pray and rely on God in situations that may be uncomfortable for her. We can tap into her brilliant brain and her uncanny ability to memorize things to help her learn scripture and worship songs to fulfill her desire to become a worship leader one day. We can teach her that her diagnosis does not limit her, but in fact gives her an advantage because her brain can hold tremendous amounts of information. She is still on several waiting lists for ABA therapy, but that does not mean that we cannot learn everything we can about it to help her at home.

With Ashley, I knew that there was no one else I could rely on, other than my parents and God. It was my sole responsibility to provide for her financially and emotionally guide her. It was all on my shoulders. I parented out of fear and tried to prevent every possible mistake before she could make it. I could be described as an octopus parent instead of a helicopter parent because hovering wasn't close enough. I was a baby raising a baby, and I had no idea what I was doing. I just knew that I did not want her to be hurt, make the mistakes I did, or get caught up in a world that I narrowly escaped. Parenting out of fear and overcontrolling each situation is not a good thing, and I certainly wouldn't want any child to have to be parented that way. I have apologized over and over to her, and now we laugh about it. My phrase when she was growing up was "one bad decision will change the course of your life." While this is true, the idea that I could prevent her from being hurt or afraid to make a decision without consulting me has caused much work for both of us as she got older. I probably got it wrong more than I got it right, but what never wavered was my love for her and my indescribable desire to give her a life better than I could dream. Typing this out, I recognize it's all about me and what I could do; it was me protecting and guiding her. God was nowhere to be found in my parenting style.

As I moved forward through life, it became abundantly clear that the things that I walked through had purpose. God used each and every mistake to help me or someone else through my sharing a piece of how God moved in and through my life. While I generally didn't see it at the time, God always had a plan, was there when I would veer off track, and was lovingly waiting to show me how I could use whatever situation it was to help myself or someone else. Being a mother was certainly one of these things. Once Rich came into my life, I was no longer carrying the weight of the world on my shoulders. We learned to work together, and the stability that came as we grew in our faith became more apparent to everyone, including ourselves. While we still stress and second-guess ourselves sometimes, we find it easier to talk through things, pray, and make decisions together.

It seems the more children we had, the more laid back I became. I'm pretty sure this is because when you have a little herd of children, attempting to control every move is only something that God can do. Ashley laughs now when she comes home from college and often comments about how she would never get away with some of the things the littles do now, and she is completely right. Learning to trust Him with them, guiding them the best we know how, and resting in His promises has become easier as our faith has deepened.

Ashley is an absolutely amazing woman, completely brilliant, beautiful, and thriving at college. That statement goes to show that no matter how badly we feel we did as a parent, God is the ultimate director and can help to make things right. When we seek Him first and pray, then the need for control and anxious feelings can slowly be replaced with the confidence to trust decisions we make and peace that can only come from Him. When I tell people that we have six children, the phrase, "I don't know how you do it," is the easiest one to respond to. The only way we get through is with Jesus and a lot of coffee!

Through allowing Jesus to move in me, I also became a different person in the process. The short-tempered, easily irritated version of me slowly became extremely patient, wanting to help others through understanding and discernment. My mother often comments that I am a different person, but I disagree (respectfully) with her. I am the same person, made new in Him. Other people will always see me as the 17-year-old pregnant girl with the drug addict boyfriend. That's fine because my approval does not come from them. It does make me sad sometimes that those people will miss out on knowing the real me because of preconceived ideas that they can't let go of. Learning to not let others' opinions of me impact me with how I feel about myself has been such a huge part of my transformation. It is through the trials, heartaches, loss, and one bad decision after another that I was slowly formed into the woman I am today. I am not ashamed of who I am or my past and my scars, and if it helps one person in their walk with God, then it was all worth it. If not, it was still worth it because I learned who He was, is, and will always be. No matter what, I know that He is there.

My role as a mother is to help create and guide our children to love the Lord, to be good humans, and to walk in the path that is set before them. As I transition back into the workplace this year, life will get a little busier, our schedules will be full, and there will be big changes for each of us. I have enjoyed my time as a stay-at-home mom, but it was clear that that season was ending, and God created the perfect position for me. Our children will be able to go back to the Christian school that they were able to attend in the past, and I will be working at the school. To say I am extremely thankful and blessed with this opportunity is an understatement. Seasons change and end to make way for the new seasons to come. To take the next steps of the path God set before me with my children is teaching them to trust God's plan. I would like to think that parents want their children to know that no matter where their path leads them, or if they wander down a wrong path, they will never be alone. God will always be there first and foremost, and they are to turn to Him first, but their parents will also be there for them, too. While I pray for their current situations, I also pray for their transitions and different stages of life, for their future spouses, for their children, and for the impact they will have on the world. While I hope and pray they are all successful, the greatest parenting goals that we have is for them is to be Christ-like in their relationships and actions and for them sharing the love of God with others. It's so easy to become fixated on careers, finances, and status, but none of it will matter if they do not have the Lord. The three things to fill in the blanks, find the answers with, and to solve our problems aren't things at all. The answer is three in one; the Father, Son, and Holy Spirit. If we have God, He will provide the answers to the blanks the world says we need to find.

Our kids often complain about us having to do schoolwork on the weekends or throughout the week. We explained that we are following the path that God set before us, which also means that we are completing our educations later than a lot of other people. They see us working hard and the value of education. We want them to know that no matter the challenges faced in life, obstacles, or diagnosis given, God has a plan for their lives.

You see, Rich did not graduate high school and college was not something that he felt was in the cards for him. He had created this idea that he was not smart enough and he wouldn't be successful. When we started dating, he was nearing the end of his military career and we were discussing his next steps. He was able to find a wonderful job doing pretty much the same thing he was doing in the Navy, but as a contractor. I began to encourage him to go to school. He not only went to school to get his bachelor's degree, but he did so while working full-time and having an infant, and while

I was also in school. He did all of that and still graduated with an awesome GPA.

There were many reasons for him to stop with his bachelor's degree. That itself was quite the accomplishment considering the timing and everything we had going on. But, he knew that God had called him to pursue a master of divinity in pastoral counseling. This meant another ninety-six credit hours that he would have to complete. Once he made the decision to complete it, quitting was not an option. It was hard, and there were many times quitting seemed like the easiest, best solution, but the little voices encouraging him to keep going and reassuring him that he could do it was all the motivation that he needed.

This year was a milestone year for us as he went on to graduate from seminary, he turned forty, and we celebrated our ten-year wedding anniversary. While we certainly believe in working hard, we feel it is equally important to play hard and pour into our relationship. The children have learned about perseverance and finishing what they start through his example.

They know, because we talk about it, the importance of Rich and I spending time together to pour into our relationship. It has become harder to get away as the number of children has increased, but we try as often as possible to not only date each other, but to also have individual dates with the children. Spending that quality time with them one-on-one allows for conversations that would not normally happen because other kids are around. We can speak into them specifically and intentionally and show them how important they are.

With the exception of a cruise for our five-year anniversary, which was also our honeymoon, Rich and I had not taken a trip without the children. As Ashley's junior year of college was fast approaching, she encouraged us to do something to celebrate all of the milestones of the year. She knew that internships would be coming, as well as plans to travel abroad for college courses. With Andrea's diagnosis and just the number of children we had, leaving them was a big deal, and there was no one else we would feel comfortable leaving the children with, other than Ashley. We decided that we would take her up on it, and we planned a trip to Ireland. My mother and stepfather joined us. It was absolutely magical and more beautiful than words can say. I am so thankful for the time we were able to spend with them and with each other. It also set an example for our children the importance of dating your spouse and making one another a priority.

I think travel can be just like with children, if you wait until you are ready or have enough money, you may never get there. With us, we don't really have extra money, but I am great about stocking money away and letting it build up over time. We saved for years to be able to take this vacation, and while the money certainly could have gone to other things, the time we spent together and with my mom and stepdad was priceless. The trip to Ireland, my new job, and Rich finishing seminary were all pieces in our puzzle this past year. All of these things, just like Andrea's diagnosis and everything in our lives, happened in His time.

CHAPTER 15
Fearfully and Wonderfully Made

*H*ave you heard the phrase, "Jack of all trades, master of none"? That's how I feel most of the time. I have bounced around from one thing to the next, never really finding my purpose. To name a few of the jobs I have had: retail store, fast food (which I don't even know if it counts because I only worked there for three hours), pizza store, pretzel shop, 911 dispatcher for two different cities, temporary worker for medical centers, front desk receptionist at a free clinic, laboratory processing specialist, nail technician, (regrettably) telemarketer, insurance agent, contractor for the government, procurement specialist for a large ship repair company, background investigator, volunteer at church as a group leader and women's group leader, volunteer with the counseling center, and, lastly, a stay-at-home mom. I am quite certain that I have forgotten some things, but I think I made the point pretty well. I never had a problem finding or keeping a job. I was always chasing the next thing, looking for more, or just never feeling like it was the right fit. That was, until I became a mom and discovered that, while it is the hardest job I have ever had, it is the most rewarding and important one that I will ever have.

Not only am I a jack of all trades, but I'd like to believe I'm pretty good at giving recommendations, too. It is comical now with my friends that when someone needs a recommendation or some type of repair, or is not sure who to call, they call me because I know everyone for something, or I know how to find someone if I don't know them personally. I believe in supporting my friends and their businesses, and certain things just stick. Do you need an electrician, plumber, or handyman? Depending on who you are and what it is, my husband may just show up at your door to fix it because I asked him to. Do you need a coupon, counselor, or glass technician? So many things, I've got you covered. It's because I like to, no, I am programmed internally and can't stop myself from trying to help people. If I am unable to help personally, I want nothing more than to be able to help them fix their issue quickly. I am a helper, and it just comes naturally. This is a part of my puzzle that God created, and if you don't have those pieces, then it doesn't mean anything other than it's not your puzzle and that is okay. We have to accept that we all have challenges and don't always know where our puzzle pieces fit just yet. When we can take those challenges and seek God, pray, and trust Him by controlling our reactions to them, that is where victory is found. It isn't what happens to us, but how we choose to react in those moments and use the lessons we've learned in the past to help us through the current situation.

It is never too late for someone to turn their life around and back to Jesus. He is the foundation and rock from which everything else comes. I am not just a stay-at-home mom. I am not limited by a box that society wants to put me in. I am so much more because I am His child, and so are you. If no one has ever told you; your worth, value, importance, acceptance, validation, accomplishments, mistakes, education, job title, promotion, clothing size, vehicle, children's successes, children's mistakes, abuse, scars, victories, or any other label you or someone else has placed on you does not define you. If you ever have doubts, turn to His word.

Psalm 139:13-18 says, "For you created my inmost being; you knit me together in my mother's womb. I praise you because I am fearfully and wonderfully made; your works are wonderful, I know that full well. My frame was not hidden from you when I was made in the secret place, when I was woven together in the depths of the earth. Your eyes saw my unformed body; all the days ordained for me were written in your book before one of them came to be. How precious to me are your thoughts, God! How vast is the sum of them! Were I to count them, they would outnumber the grains of sand - when I awake, I am still with you."

Erasing years of negative self-talk, labels that others have given us, and feeling less than does not magically just go away. Sometimes it comes in the form of you allowing God to change you, transform you, and become a new person, even if old friends or even family are unable to accept the changes and will continue to see you as the old you. That is not your fault, and there is nothing you can do for them other than pray for them. It is up to God to change others, and it is up to them to let their walls down, stop being judgmental or holding on to the past, and allow the Holy Spirit to transform their thoughts and minds.

I have met with so many women who are so hurt, not by friends or outsiders, but by family. They share the passive aggressive tendencies to dance around issues and gossip about each other instead of acting like family. Seeing women so broken by those who are supposed to love them most is disheartening. They have to learn that you cannot change someone's opinion of you, and you can't stop the words that come out of their mouths, but you can set healthy boundaries for yourself and limit the exposure you have to them. For some, friends become the family that you choose and are the ones who are there when actual family is too busy talking about you instead of being there for you.

Prayer, positive self-talk, and surrounding yourself with people who can remind you of those things even when it is hard to see will make a tremendous difference. God can make all things new, and there is nothing impossible for him. I have been guilty of labeling one of my children as shy. She has picked this up and is often hesitant to try new things because she believes she is shy. We started changing the way that we talked to her and about her and started using words like caring and compassionate. We tell her she is important and that while it may be a little difficult to try new things, she can do this. Her confidence is growing, her desire to put herself into more situations where she may feel a bit timid is increasing, and that label that we had stuck on her is being peeled off. While everyone is created differently, being mindful about labeling each other, creating unrealistic expectations, and placing limitations on someone is not okay. Repeating who you are in Christ is a wonderful way to change that mindset. When all else fails, Jesus never will.

Life is short, it is but a blink of an eye in the overall picture. We have the unique opportunity to share the love of Jesus through our words and actions. If you are sharing about God with one breath and gossiping about what someone wore to church in the next breath, what message are you sending to unbelievers? If you believe in the forgiveness of sin, all sin, from God, yet hold on to grudges and unforgiveness about things that don't ultimately matter, what are you teaching a generation that is watching and learning from you? If you believe God can forgive others sin, yet can't accept that He forgives your sin, I ask that you seek His heart and genuine love for you. There is nothing that you have to do to earn the love of Jesus. He loves you because you are His chosen favorite. We are all equal in His eyes. We are all loved by Him. We are all His beloved. We are all created by Him to be our own puzzle piece in the beautiful masterpiece that He created. We have our own unique look and shape and fit perfectly in our own place. Once we can accept and hold our own piece, then it is easier to find where we fit. Don't try to take someone's piece or damage the edges to the pieces that fit together with ours. While the outside may become frayed, bent, worn, or faded, the center remains whole and unchanging, because it is Christ that centers us. Once our worn pieces connect with others, we begin to see the bigger picture. While individually each piece is beautiful and wonderfully made, watching the puzzle come together is stunning.

I encourage you to find your surrounding pieces, connect, make a difference, and create something beautiful that only you can. Asking for help during the process is not a sign of weakness. In fact, it is a sign of great strength. For me, I forced my piece into ones that didn't fit many times with different groups of friends. It was easy to pretend that it fit for a while, but the more I looked at it, it just wasn't right. It's a bit harder to take the piece out, but once you know it's not right, it's got to come out. You know when you may have outgrown friends or people that you have felt comfortable with in the past. Once you know that it's time to move forward, it can be difficult, but in the end, it's the right choice. You do not have to stay stuck with the wrong friend pieces. It may take some time to find your group, or you may have the same tight circle of friends. Either way, we were created to do life together and in relationship with others.

Together we have the ability to do so much more than we ever could individually. Let's use this one life we were given to make an impact for good and be the change for our children and for generations to come.

CHAPTER 16
Words of Wisdom

I don't know everything, not even close, but I have learned a whole lot since I was that 17-year-old pregnant girl. There are many lessons that God has given me over and over until I finally understand and learn from the situations. I have spent countless hours in prayer, studying and researching topics that are important to me, learning from professionals who have a wealth of information, and having people in my life that can be trusted for spiritual advice and guidance.

Let God be God! When it comes to saving someone, only God can do that. I have tried giving ultimatums, drawn bottom lines, and risked my life in an effort to save someone else. While I often felt like I was the only one who had done this or something similar, I found that it was extremely common, just not talked about. It is a false belief that we can save someone else. In fact, that is so far from the truth that it can be dangerous. If I can just get through to one woman, one teenage girl, one innocent life, then everything that I went through trying to save my drug-addicted boyfriend was all worth it. Putting the importance and safety of someone else's life above your own will not only give you a false sense of security, but it will also slowly destroy the essence of who you are and were created to be. There can be only one savior, and He is more than capable.

Words Have Power! Words can provide comfort, or cut

someone to the core. Thinking about what you are actually saying, or are about to say, can help you provide words of encouragement in hard times versus amplify someone's emotional pain. When it comes to what to say and what not to say when someone suffers a miscarriage, infertility, or any type of loss, it can be so hard to know what to say and how to say it. In the instance of a miscarriage, you may encounter someone who has not yet heard the news, they may awkwardly congratulate you, you may not know how to respond, and you both end up feeling terrible. This happened to me on several occasions. This is not the fault of the person not knowing. It is just a situation that happens more often than not. When the person finds out, they typically feel terrible about bringing it up, and the one who had the loss has to continue to relive the situation. Here, there is much room for grace and an opportunity to provide prayers and support. Often, the person going through it does not know what they need. That is okay, for both of you. A reassuring word of "I'm so sorry", "I am here for you", "I love you", "How can I pray for you?", or "Can I pray for you right now?" can do so much for someone hurting. I found that many people would avoid me, not out of disrespect, but because they did not know what to say. It is okay to be honest and let the person know that you do not know exactly what to say, but that you are there with them and they are not alone.

Grief and loss are experienced in different ways; no two people grieve exactly the same, and it can come and go and can continue to resurface after weeks, months, or years. Healing takes time, and there were several times where I was told to just get over it and move on. No one has the authority to tell someone else how fast they should heal or have expectations of what someone's healing should look like. It is made worse when those we love and frequently see do not acknowledge the grief or loss and pretend that it never happened. A simple hug can do more than a million words sometimes.

On the other side of the fence, there are things that were said to me that stung. I would suggest rewording comments like, "I know exactly how you are feeling." This one was especially frustrating for me because I didn't even know how I was feeling. How in the world could someone, someone I barely knew mind you, know exactly what that was? Empathy for someone is one thing; comparison, assumptions, and minimization of your grief is another thing. The other comments that hurt to the core were, "You are so strong; I could never handle that," "Look on the bright side," "You can always try again for another one," "It's probably for the best," 'There was probably something wrong with them," "At least you have one child already," 'They are in a better place," and the ever common, "Everything happens for a reason." While these comments are usually well-meaning, they can hurt. For me, the losses were very difficult, and Rich and I had to process the emotions in our own way. The friends who were there to pray and just listen were the ones we turned to. We have had a total of four miscarriages and each was equally as painful because we lost a child.

When I talked to my midwife about it, I truly had no idea how common it was, and she shared with me that the average number of miscarriages to pregnancy was one in four. This tells me that many couples grieve in silence, keeping their pain unknown to those outside. Suffering in silence can be a lonely place, and sharing with others, maybe not through a social media outlet if that is not your thing, but within your safe group of close friends, allows for a safe place to grieve and gives others the opportunity to pray for you.

Be the Church. What does it mean to be the church? By church I do not mean the actual building where you attend, but rather Christians uniting as one to share the love and hope of Jesus. In fact, Galatians 5:22-23 explains that when we live our lives with Jesus, we are filled with love, joy, peace, patience, kindness, goodness, faithfulness, gentleness, and self-control, or Fruit of the Spirit. Are the actions we display today reflective of these traits, or are they more reflective of hate, fear, war, impatience, rudeness, arrogance, judgment, harshness, and lashing out? While attending church on Sundays is important, it is the actual relationships that are formed from doing life together and creating an atmosphere of transparency, growing together in His word, that make the church thrive.

I have witnessed how investing in the life of someone can change the path and direction of their life. Spending time with the elderly, learning and soaking in the wisdom they have to impart can be life-changing. When I was on a mission trip to Haiti, I had the privilege to sit and talk with the oldest woman in the small village we were visiting. I asked her to please share with me one thing that she learned throughout her lifetime that she wished everyone could know. She sat there, processing my question, taking her time to answer, and slowly a smile began to appear. She reached out for my hand and pulled me down so that we were eye to eye. With tears in her eyes, she said love of God and others is the most valuable lesson anyone could ever know. It all comes back to love.

Love can be shown in so many different ways and areas. Love can be helping your neighbor, not because you have to, but because you want to. Love can be caring for children because you want them to be in a safe and loving environment. Love can be not letting someone on the street go hungry, but offer food without wondering what their intentions are. Love can be intentional about having relationships with people who have differing views, opinions, and backgrounds from you. Love can be showing up when your friend is in the middle of a crisis, armed with coffee and a hug, just to be there. Just love. Be the Church.

Testify! There is power in your testimony, and sharing it with someone can change his or her life as much as it has your own. His timing is not for us to know or understand; yet, it is always perfect. Through Rich's powerful testimony, he has been able to share with others facing similar situations, and where there is light, darkness cannot hide. Through years of prayer, understanding addiction, and his willingness to be transparent and vulnerable, God freed him, and we are forever thankful and so blessed. If you or someone you love is struggling with addiction, there is help available, and the same can be true for you. God has not and will never leave your side. No matter what you are facing, with His help, you can get through it. Running from it, hiding it, or avoiding it does not make it go away; it just causes isolation, feelings of loneliness, depression, anxiety, anger, and you fill in the blank for yourself. It does not have to be twelve steps, or even three, just one. One brave step to get help, one brave prayer crying out to God to save you because you know He is the only one who can, one brave conversation with your spouse, one brave "me too" when someone shares what they are facing in a small group, one brave step to go to a meeting that you've been making excuses not to go to, or one brave step to pray for your spouse who is in the middle of the battle is all it takes. One brave moment of vulnerability with God can cause your chains to fall in an instant. It just takes one brave moment to listen to those who love you tell you hard things that you do not want to hear and one brave moment to surrender. Be brave and testify!

Leave a Legacy! What kind of legacy are you leaving? As we get older and our parents get older, our roles as children may shift and take on different forms. Many people these days are finding the need to become caretakers for their parents. You do what needs to be done, no matter the difficulty, for the best interest of the ones you love. That may mean a nursing home, assisted living, hiring a nurse, building an addition to have them move in with you, buying a new home, or whatever makes the most sense for your family. When I was entering high school, my parents sold the home we were living in and bought a home less than a mile away in another neighborhood. You would have thought that we moved to another country with how I reacted. I was not happy, did not want to move, and was quite the brat. Fast forward many years, I am so thankful for the time that we had with my grandparents and the lessons they were able to share with me and later on with my children. My grandfather was larger than life and had a smile and laugh that was contagious. The love he shared for each of his children and grandchildren was unexplainable, and he was able to make each one of us feel special.

While their presence can never be replaced and we miss them

more than words can say, the impact they had on generations will be felt forever. The legacy they left is one to be admired. To have known them was to love them, and they inspire me every day to be a better person. In a time when life was hard, they clung to the most important things: faith, family, and helping others. Why do we complicate things so much these days? Is it too far-fetched to think that we could go back to the days of neighbor helping neighbor, seeing a need of others and filling the need, and always having room at the table for whoever comes over?

No, we did not plan on having a large family. Yes, we love big, it's so loud sometimes that we can barely hear ourselves think. It often seems like a toy store exploded all over our house, but we love it. The biggest question that I get is how do we do it? How do we raise six children in today's world? The biggest piece of advice is to plan, prep, and plan some more. Things run so much smoother when I preplan our meals for the month. It is more cost effective when I plan our grocery lists and shopping. While we have not perfected it yet, having a schedule for laundry and chores to help around the house teaches the kids responsibility and ownership of their things. Honestly, it is a lot like herding cats, just trying to stay one step ahead of them. Our children are now 20, 9, 8, 6, 4, and 2. When I am so tired that I do not feel like I can even take another step, I ask God to give me strength. When I do not have the words to say, I ask God to give me wisdom. When I feel completely overwhelmed and out of control, I ask God for peace that only He can give.

The reality is, I can do nothing on my own without Him, and I do not want to. Having God in the center of my life, helping me to forgive all the sins of my youth and sins of today, is what keeps me grounded. It takes placing Him in the center of my marriage as we grow together to be an example for others of what a Godly union is. It requires releasing control and allowing Him to be the center of my relationships, the unexpected and the ones who have become family, which allows for transparency, vulnerability, and a deeper relationship with one another, but more importantly, with

God. It takes having those God-given friends who make you laugh until your cheeks hurt, wipe your tears when you are hurting, and will tell you when you have something in your teeth, feeling safe to remove those filters and be real.

While it does not seem like it when you are in the thick of raising children, one day they will be grown up and out of the house. Taking time to invest in your marriage not only honors God by placing your spouse first, but also invests in your future together. Date nights do not have to be expensive and should not be a reason or an excuse as to why you do not have them. They can be at home, after the kids go to bed, just spending quality time together. It is the effort that matters and will continue to matter as the years go on.

Facing a diagnosis, whether it is autism or a terminal illness, for yourself, your child, or someone you love is no surprise to God, and He will be beside you, as the constant that will remain through each blink, no matter what. When you feel alone, turn to Him. As we navigate this path with Andrea, we will turn to God first and help her learn how she can honor Him with her life. The puzzle pieces of her life have not changed in God's eyes, and they will still fit together beautifully, no matter what, because she is His child first.

Be still, and He will guide and awaken you. No matter what happens in life, everything can change in the blink of an eye, yet God is the constant that will remain through each blink.

CPSIA information can be obtained
at www.ICGtesting.com
Printed in the USA
BVHW030420061219
565805BV00001B/20/P